PAPER BOUQUET

Paper Bouquet

Using Paper Punches to Create Beautiful Flowers

By **Susan Tierney Cockburn**

LARK BOOKS

A Division of Sterling Publishing Co., Inc.
New York / London

SENIOR EDITOR: Valerie Van Arsdale Shrader

EDITOR: Julie Hale

ART DIRECTOR: Kristi Pfeffer

COVER DESIGNER: Cindy LaBreacht

PRODUCTION: Thom Gaines

PROJECT PHOTOGRAPHY: Steve Mann

HOW-TO PHOTOGRAPHY: Doug Yaple

Library of Congress Cataloging-in-Publication Data

Cockburn, Susan Tierney.
 Paper bouquet: using paper punches to create beautiful flowers / Susan Tierney Cockburn.
   p. cm.
 ISBN-13: 978-1-60059-059-7 (pb-trade pbk. : alk. paper)
 ISBN-10: 1-60059-059-4 (pb-trade pbk. : alk. paper)
1. Paper flowers. I. Title.
 TT892.C625 2008
 745.594'3--dc22

                                    2007034170

10 9 8 7 6 5 4 3

Published by Lark Books, A Division of
Sterling Publishing Co., Inc.
387 Park Avenue South, New York, NY 10016

Text © 2008, Susan Tierney Cockburn
Photography © 2008, Lark Books unless otherwise specified
Illustrations © 2008, Lark Books unless otherwise specified

Distributed in Canada by Sterling Publishing,
c/o Canadian Manda Group, 165 Dufferin Street
Toronto, Ontario, Canada M6K 3H6

Distributed in the United Kingdom by GMC Distribution Services,
Castle Place, 166 High Street, Lewes, East Sussex, England BN7 1XU

Distributed in Australia by Capricorn Link (Australia) Pty Ltd.,
P.O. Box 704, Windsor, NSW 2756 Australia

If you have questions or comments about this book, please contact:
Lark Books
67 Broadway
Asheville, NC 28801
828-253-0467

Manufactured in China

ISBN 13: 978-1-60059-059-7

For information about custom editions, special sales, premium and corporate purchases, please contact Sterling Special Sales Department at 800-805-5489 or specialsales@sterlingpub.com.

Introduction 8

Basics 10
Materials and Tools
Construction Techniques

The Flowers 22

Amaryllis 24

Anemone 26

Aster 30

Azalea 32

Bachelor's Button 34

Begonia 36

Camellia 38

Carnation 40

Cherry Blossom 42

Chrysanthemum 44

Clematis 48

Coreopsis 50

Cosmos 52

Daffodil 54

Dogwood 58

Echinacea 60

Forsythia 62

Gardenia 64

Gerber Daisy 66

Holly and Berries 68

Impatiens 70

Iris 72

Japanese Anemone 76

Marigold 78

Ornamental Kale 82

Pansy 84

Peony 87

Periwinkle 90

Petunia 92

Pinecone 94

Poinsettia 96

Primrose 99

Queen Anne's Lace 102

Rhododendron 104

Rose 106

Sweet Pea 108

Tulip 112

Verbena 114

Violet 116

Zinnia 120

Punch Directory 124

About the author 126

Acknowledgments 126

Index 127

INTRODUCTION

I have always been drawn to flowers. The color and structure of a single blossom are, to me, marvels of nature. The first flower that made an impression on me was the dahlia. My grandmother grew prize-winning dahlias in Maryland and often took me with her to her garden club. Years later, while living in Connecticut, I combined my love of flowers with a passion for crafting. During the long, cold northeastern winters, I missed the sight of colorful blossoms. I needed a way to keep flowers in my life regardless of the season. During that time, I noticed craft punches at a stamp store and saw how their shapes resembled flower petals. That's how the seeds of these projects were planted!

My first creations were very simple. Once I got started punching, cardstock became my preferred material, because of its durability. To add dimension to each punched petal, I manipulated the cardstock with a chopstick, a stylus, or tweezers into a shape that was appropriate for the type of flower I wanted to make. Now, thanks to the variety of craft punches and sophisticated tools available, my imagination knows no boundaries when it comes to creating flowers from paper.

How did I pick the punches for these projects? I let the flowers tell me which ones to choose. I studied the real-life version of every flower featured on these pages, then broke each one of them down into its individual components. From there, I matched each separate component to an appropriate craft punch. The result is a garden full of paper blossoms that encompasses all four seasons. From daffodils and marigolds like the ones you plant in your garden, to ornamental shrubs such as rhododendron and forsythia, to holiday favorites like poinsettias and holly, the range of projects in this book reflects the variety and abundance of nature.

Browse the basics section, and you'll see just how simple it is to make the 40 flowers featured here. Everything you need to know in order to get started, including information about tools and materials, can be found in this chapter. You'll also find a detailed overview of the techniques I use for crafting with cardstock. Paper punches are fun and incredibly easy to work with. In order to make the flower-crafting process extra easy, illustrations of the punched pieces you need to create each flower accompany every project.

As a gardener, I delight in the experience of planting flowers and watching them grow. A bed of blooming flowers is proof of what's possible when you invest love and care in a project. As a crafter, I strive to replicate the joy of flowers in paper to create a lasting beauty to share with others. With *Paper Bouquet*, I hope to inspire in you that same sense of joy as you learn to make your own enchanting paper tulips, roses, and pansies. These magical blossoms have a charm that transcends the seasons and making them is easier than you think.

Creating three-dimensional flowers in paper is a wonderful way to preserve memories of your garden or replicate a favorite flower from your travels. Paper flowers also make delightful gifts—as decorative accents in a special vase, as unique and everlasting bouquets, as embellishments on gift boxes or bags. And they're perfect for making seasonal arrangements you can enjoy throughout the year.

Regardless of how you choose to use your paper flowers, I hope they inspire you and bring a smile to your face. Let your inner artist blossom!

BASICS

Getting started in three-dimensional floral paper craft is easy. The necessary materials can be found in just about any craft, stamp, or scrapbook supply store. All you need are craft punches, cardstock, a few simple tools, and glue that's suitable for working with paper. In this chapter I'll identify the punches you need to make your own paper garden. I'll also explain my innovative techniques for structuring cardstock to form petals and leaves. I urge you to familiarize yourself with these techniques, because they are the key to creating the 40 beautiful blossoms in this book.

MATERIALS AND TOOLS

Cardstock

I use 80-pound cardstock in most of my projects, because it's a sturdy material. Since cardstock is fairly durable, I don't have to worry about my dimensional blooms getting flattened. While I place some of my paper bouquets behind glass, many of my creations are made to be touched—they're given as gifts, and I want the recipients to be able to handle and enjoy them. The use of cardstock makes this possible.

Each project in this book features a list of recommended cardstock colors, but you can use just about any shade of cardstock you fancy to make these flowers. I prefer cardstock that has a slight texture or definition to it, because it gives the flower petals a detail that I don't have to add later with tools.

Paper craft punches

When I began creating paper flowers, I used simple craft punches like hearts and circles, because that's all that was available. I had to trim other shapes into petals and leaves in order to mimic the flowers in my garden. Craft punch companies eventually recognized the need for new punches and began designing them. The variety of paper craft punches has definitely grown over the years. Today the shapes are more specific. You can easily find craft punches that produce precise shapes, like the begonia petals punch or the sweet pea punch. Detail is essential to the creation of these blossoms. The inclusion of tiny particulars like a stamen or a seed head is one of the reasons my paper flowers look so lifelike.

Basic Tool Kit

Glue

I use a high-performance paper adhesive that sets in five to 10 minutes and dries clear in approximately 30 minutes. The glue creates a flexible water-resistant bond. Squeeze out about a dime-sized amount each time so you don't waste the glue.

Toothpick

This handy little tool is perfect for applying small amounts of glue to tiny paper pieces.

Rubber mat

As a work area for shaping my punched pieces, I use a firm mouse pad that's at least ¼-inch thick. I use the underside of the mouse pad, because it provides a superior surface for executing most of my paper-shaping techniques.

Art gum eraser

An art gum eraser is ideal for shaping mini or small punched pieces.

TOOL KIT CONTENTS

To complete the projects in this book, you'll need the following tools:
- Glue
- Toothpick
- Rubber mat
- Art gum eraser
- Small, medium, and large ball styluses
- Molding tool
- Small scissors
- Reverse or self-closing tweezers

It provides extra firmness for working with paper. Tiny pieces are often
more defined when shaped on an art
gum eraser.

Styluses

Styluses are required for executing several of the paper structuring
techniques that follow. I use a small
or medium ball stylus when cupping
or stirring a punched paper piece
and a large ball stylus when shaping a punched paper piece. You can

Tools for creating three-dimensional flowers include (L to R): Paper glue, mouse pad,
styluses in various sizes, small scissors, reverse tweezers (in front), standard tweezers (in
back), molding tool, punch aid tool, craft punch. The tool kit shown in back contains a stylus
and interchangeable balls, a molding tool, reverse tweezers, and some extra paper-crafting
supplies, including craft blades and a piercing tool.

purchase small, medium, and large ball styluses individually. A set with interchangeable balls in a convenient tool kit is also available.

Molding tool

A molding tool is essential for structuring punched paper shapes. I use a molding tool that has one rounded end and one concave end. Both ends are used for shaping paper pieces.

Small scissors

There are times when I need to make tiny snips in a paper shape, or trim a punched piece, and small-sized scissors are perfect for these types of tasks. I use them in practically every project.

Tweezers

I use reverse or self-closing tweezers when making my flowers. Reverse tweezers are different from the standard kind: to open a set of reverse tweezers, you squeeze the handles. To close a set of reverse tweezers, you release the handles. Reverse tweezers can serve as a third

hand or vice to hold a punched piece in place while you add glue to the piece. When working with rolled-up shapes, you can position the tweezers at the closure of the roll to secure the piece while the glue dries. You can also use reverse tweezers to grasp a punched piece while you pinch and bend it. I usually use tweezers to pick up the punched pieces I'm attaching to my flower.

Tools for adding spot color

Sometimes cardstock alone isn't enough to replicate the variety of hues both subtle and bright that are contained in a single flower. In order to more accurately re-create the rainbow colors of a carnation or a begonia, I add spot color to my punched pieces. I use several different items for adding color, depending on the specific need I have for making a flower.

Pigment ink pen

I prefer pigment ink pens to watercolor pens, because they have a longer shelf life when properly

stored, and they don't bleed. Pigment ink pens are excellent for adding detail color to punched paper pieces. I use pigment ink pens throughout this book to add color to the ends of petals. Stroking the pen over your petals will make them look more natural.

Chalk

Chalk is ideal for adding contrast to petals. I use chalk when I want to create an area of contrasting color that's soft, shaded, or highlighted. The chalks I prefer are acid-free, and they come with an applicator tool and reusable pompoms. Pompoms in three different sizes are included for each color of chalk, so that I can shade tiny areas as well as large petals.

Watercolor paints

Watercolor paints are perfect for adding dramatic color to petals. I use shimmering, pearlescent watercolor cakes that are nontoxic, acid-free, and dry quickly. It only takes a few drops of water to activate the paint. To apply the paint, I use a water brush with a reservoir.

I stroke each piece lightly with the brush to create the details I want. Watercolor paints also work well when you need to give your petals a speckled look.

Gel ink pens

Several of the flowers in this book have petals or stamens with characteristics that are too small to re-create with a punch. In order to reproduce those fine details, I use gel ink pens. The Pansy project (page 84), for example, features distinctive lines that are drawn on each petal using a gel ink pen. If I'm working with a cardstock that's dark—deep purple, black, or red—I

use gel pens that are especially made for coloring on dark material. Another advantage of gel ink pens is that you can use them to apply several coats of color to your paper pieces, a technique that creates extra dimension.

Glitter glue or liquid pearls

There are times when I want to accentuate the center of a flower, and glitter glue does the trick. Applying small dabs to several areas on the center of a flower is a great way to replicate the bracts of a dogwood, the flower of a poinsettia, or the center of a periwinkle.

CONSTRUCTION TECHNIQUES

Cupping

This is a very easy technique to master. To cup a punched piece, start by placing it on the rubber mouse pad or the art gum eraser. With the small or medium ball stylus placed at a 90° angle to the paper, firmly press down on the center of the piece. The piece will be drawn upward, naturally, forming the cup shape that gave this technique its name.

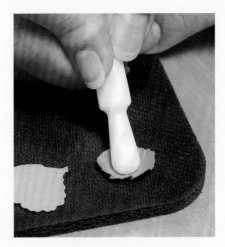

An exception to this one-step cupping technique occurs when a punched piece has a large surface area in the middle. A sun shape is a good example. With this type of paper piece, it's necessary to release the surface tension of the shape prior to cupping it. To do this, use the small scissors to snip between each ray of the sun. Then cup the shape with the stylus.

Shaping

I refer to this technique as shaping, but it's actually a method for conditioning cardstock so that it's easy to manipulate later with the other techniques. You'll find that the cardstock softens drastically with these shaping techniques. You can use either end of the molding tool or the large ball stylus for shaping pieces.

With simple shapes like circles or large punched pieces, the rounded end of the molding tool works great.

To shape a punched piece, place it on the rubber mouse pad and press down on it with the ball end of the molding tool. Then move the tool back and forth or in a circular motion to soften the cardstock. If a punched piece has detail to it or is very small—a piece used as an individual petal, for example—use the concave, half-moon shape of the molding tool or the large ball stylus to shape it. Simply place the punched piece on the rubber mouse pad, place your index finger on the flat side of the piece, then rub the tool or stylus back and forth over the shape to soften it.

To pinch a petal from a one-shaped punch like the daisy, place the tweezers about ¼ inch in from the outer part of the petal, then use your thumb and index finger to press the shape around the tweezers.

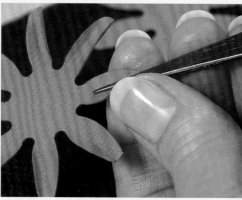

If you're using a large ball stylus, just rub it back and forth over the piece, as if you were erasing a mistake. For creating the petals used in the Tulip (page 112) and Peony (page 87) projects, you should stroke downward on each petal with the stylus to condition the cardstock.

Pinching

This technique is helpful when you're constructing a flower from individual petals or shaping the petals that come from a daisy punch. In the case of individual petals, you should always pinch the smaller, defined end of the petal. This is the end that will be glued to the flower base.

Bending

This technique is frequently used in conjunction with pinching. After pinching a petal, transfer the shape to your free hand and hold it by its pinched end with your thumb and index finger. Then use the reverse tweezers to grasp the other end of the petal and bend it downward or inward. This technique gives the petal more definition.

Stirring

This technique imitates the counterclockwise stirring motion used to combine ingredients in cooking. I usually use a stylus to execute this technique. However, if the punched piece is large, I use the round end of the molding tool. To stir a shape, place the punched piece on the rubber mouse pad, then place the stylus in the center of the piece. Grasp the stylus as you would a wooden spoon and move it in a stirring motion, pressing down with the stylus as you stir. The shape will cup upward and enclose the stylus.

As with the cupping technique, if the center surface area of a punched piece is too large, you should use the small scissors to make cuts toward the center of the piece prior to stirring.

Making stems and veins

A flower simply wouldn't be complete without the appropriate leaves. To add a stem to a punched-out leaf, you should place the leaf wrong-side up on the rubber mouse pad, then use the small ball stylus to draw a stem line down the center of the piece, pressing down slightly as you move the stylus over the shape.

To add veins, turn the leaf right-side up and use the small ball stylus to draw lines from the stem line outward.

Once you've added the stem and veins to the leaf, pinch the end of the leaf that will be attached to the flower, then bend the leaf back and forth to accentuate the stem line.

You can also bend the outer end of the leaf to further naturalize its appearance.

Gluing

I use specific methods for gluing. It's important that you use these methods when you're making your own punched paper flowers. When layering punched pieces together, you should use a minimal amount of glue. By using a toothpick, you can easily apply just the right amount of glue to the bottom of a punched piece. You should never use an excessive amount of glue, as the seepage might pull the paper pieces down.

If you're constructing a flower, petal-by-petal, as in the Peony project (page 87), you can be more liberal with the amount of glue you use. With this type of project, you can dip the end of the punched piece into a glob of the glue, then attach the piece to the base.

You should hold the piece in place with the tweezers or use the art gum eraser as a rest until the glue sets enough to hold up the petal.

Rolling

Many of the centers, or stamens, made for the flowers in this book feature a rolled-up punched piece—usually a sun—that is used to create depth. To prepare a piece for rolling, use the small scissors to cut the piece two-thirds of the way through the center. Then use the reverse tweezers to hold the right side of the piece while it rests on the middle finger of your opposite hand.

Hold the tweezers at an angle of approximately 45°, then rotate the tweezers counterclockwise, so that the piece is formed into a cone.

Use the toothpick to apply a small amount of glue to the end of the roll before closing up the punched shape.

Hold the closed shape between your thumb and index finger for a few seconds so the glue can set. As mentioned above, the sun is the shape most frequently rolled in these projects. However, in the Pompom Chrysanthemum project (page 44), a small daisy is rolled into a cone to complete the center of the flower.

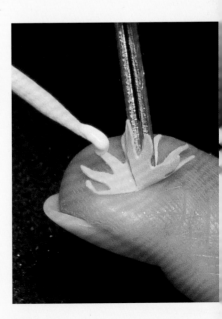

ADDITIONAL TIPS

Here are some extra hints for creating punched paper blooms.

Try using scraps of cardstock for punching your shapes—especially the stamens. This is a good way for you to use up leftover cardstock from other projects. Scraps are perfect for punching small pieces. I sort all of my cardstock by color into stackable bins, so it's readily available for use.

I like to keep a supply of punched pieces on hand and ready to use. To organize my punched pieces, I sort them out and store them in plastic bead containers. I label the containers with a marker so that I know exactly what pieces I have to work with.

For extra ease and precision when punching your paper pieces, try using a punch aid tool. You can use this tool with all sizes and shapes of craft punches. The device has a base that holds templates, depending on the size of punch you need. It also has a sturdy lever that you can press down on instead of using the palm of your hand.

To reduce the wear and tear on your punches, try using a craft punch lubricant. Available in spray form, this lubricant can help prolong the life of your punches.

To save both time and material, try cutting your cardstock into strips that are the width of the pieces

you're punching. This technique can be especially helpful when you're using a theme punch that contains many elements, and you only need one of the parts from the punch. Just turn the theme punch over, place the strip of paper under the part of the punch you need, and punch away.

When attaching petals to a shape, hold the shape in place with one hand using the small ball stylus. This keeps the base shape cupped and steady while you add petals with your other hand.

Store your glue capped and upside-down in a container. The glue flows easily when stored this way—you won't have to squeeze the bottle to get the adhesive to come out.

USING THIS BOOK

Peruse these pages, and you'll notice that the punches required to make each flower are shown in the tools and materials lists. With certain multi-part punches and theme punches—the super giant moth orchid, or the begonia petals, for instance—you won't need every piece that's punched in order to complete the flower. The multi-part punches and theme punches are illustrated in their entirety in the Punch Directory on page 124, along with a list of the flowers each punch is used for.

A gallery of unique and innovative craft ideas that let you showcase your paper blossoms is interspersed throughout this book. Once you've cultivated your flowers, you'll see how easy it is to incorporate them into other creative projects with just a little glue. From frames and hats to cards and scrapbooks and more, you'll find that paper flowers make the perfect embellishment for just about any accessory. They're a festive addition to holiday ornaments and the perfect finishing touch for a wedding album. The possibilities abound. I encourage you to think outside the vase when decorating with these beautiful blooms.

THE FLOWERS

From asters to zinnias and everything in between, all of your favorite flowers can be found in the section that follows. Perfect for use in other craft projects, these lifelike blossoms are incredibly easy to make. In the blink of an eye, you can create your own paper bouquet—flowers that are always fresh and colorful, no matter what the season.

AMARYLLIS

Also known as the knight's star lily, the amaryllis is made up of six petals in varying patterns. The red variety is the most popular, but you can replicate other types by using paint or chalk to color the cardstock.

Level of difficulty: ✿ ✿

Punches for flower and quantity needed

6 mega giant dahlia petals [a]
(For punch key and individual pieces used, see page 124.)

1 large snowflake for base of flower [b]

1 mini star for base of stamen [c]

1 jumbo sparkle for stamen [d]

Punch for leaves and quantity needed

4–6 mega elongated leaves [e]
(For punch key and individual pieces used, see page 124.)

a b c d e

Tools and Supplies

Basic Tool Kit (page 11)

Recommended cardstock:

 White, and shades of red and crimson for petals and snowflake

 Bright yellow for small star

 Yellow or white for jumbo sparkle

 Shades of green from bright to medium for leaves

Pearlescent watercolor paint in red

Pigment ink pens in red and brownish yellow

Chalk in bright green

Water reservoir brush

To make the flower

1 Punch the mega giant dahlia petals six times to produce 30 shapes. You will only use the six largest petals. Use the small scissors to round the tips of the six petals.

2 If you are making a white flower that's edged in red, use the red pigment ink pen to shade the edges of all of the petals, then use the bright green chalk to shade the center of the petal. If you choose to make a red flower with white streaks, start with the white cardstock and use the red pearlescent watercolor paint to brush red streaks down the petals.

3 Place the large snowflake on the rubber mat and use the large ball stylus to cup it, following the instructions for cupping on page 15.

4 Place the six petals on the rubber mat and use the round end of the large ball stylus to shape them (refer to page 15 for shaping techniques).

5 Pinch and bend each of the petals, following the instructions for pinching and bending on page 16.

6 Place the snowflake on the rubber mat and use the small ball stylus to secure it. Then use the tweezers to pick up one of the petals, dip the stem of the petal into the glue, and place it on one of the snowflake projections about ¼ inch (6 mm) from the center. Add the next two petals using the same technique and skipping a snowflake projection in between each petal.

7 Use the small ball stylus to hold the large snowflake securely on the rubber mat while you use the tweezers to pick up another petal. Dip the stem of the petal into the glue, then place it on one of the snowflake projections, in between two petals, and almost on the center of the snowflake. Repeat this step with the last two petals, positioning them in between the first three petals.

8 Place the small star on the art gum eraser and use the small ball stylus to cup it. Hold the shape with the tweezers and use the toothpick to dab a small amount of glue on the bottom of it. Then place the piece in the center of the flower.

9 If you are making a red flower, punch a yellow jumbo sparkle. Use the red pigment ink pen to color the sparkle, leaving about ⅛ inch (3 mm) at the tip yellow. Use the brownish yellow pigment ink pen to add some shading to the yellow tips. If you are making a white flower, punch a white jumbo sparkle. Use the bright green chalk to add some shading at the base, then use the brownish yellow pigment ink pen to tip the ends.

10 Use the small scissors to cut the sparkle projections in half. Place the jumbo sparkle on the art gum eraser and use the small ball stylus to cup it. With the toothpick, dab a small amount of glue on the center, then use your index finger and thumb to close the shape at the base. Hold the piece for a few seconds to set it. Then fluff out the projections with your free hand. Dip the base into the glue and set it on top of the small star.

11 Punch the mega elongated leaves two times to produce a total of six leaves. Place four to six of the leaves right-side down on the rubber mat. Use the small ball stylus to create a stem line down the center of each of the leaves. Shape as desired (refer to page 15 for shaping techniques). Set the flower in place on your project, then tuck the leaves under it to finish. You may need to prop up the longer leaves with the art gum eraser until they set.

ANEMONE

Part of the buttercup family, the anemone blooms in the spring and summer. Its name comes from the Greek word anemos, *which means wind, so the blossom is known to many gardeners as the windflower.*

Level of difficulty:

Punches for flower and quantity needed
1 medium snowflake for base of flower [a]
1 medium starfish [b]
11 large ovoid petals for flower [c]
2 medium delicate snowflakes for stamen [d]
1 small sun for stamen [e]
1 small snowflake for stamen [f]

Punch for leaves and quantity needed
3–4 medium ivy leaves [g]

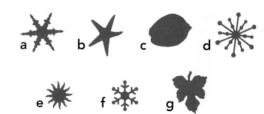

Tools and Supplies
Basic Tool Kit (page 11)
Recommended cardstock:
  Medium green for medium snowflake, starfish, and ivy leaves
  Pink, red, blue, or white for ovoid petals
  Black for medium delicate snowflakes, small snowflake, and small sun
Chalk in a shade that's deeper than flower

ANEMONE

To make the flower

1 Place the green medium snow-flake and the starfish on the rubber mat and use the large ball stylus to cup them, following the instructions for cupping on page 15. Then set the pieces aside.

2 Use the chalk to shade the center of the 11 ovoid petals. Then place the petals on the rubber mat and use the round end of the molding tool or large ball stylus to shape them (refer to page 15 for shaping techniques). Pinch and bend each of the petals, following the instructions for pinching and bending on page 16.

3 Place the green medium snow-flake on the rubber mat. Use the tweezers to pick up one of the petals and dip the pinched end of it into the glue. Then use the small ball stylus to hold the medium snowflake in place while you adhere the rest of the petals to the snow-

flake's projections. Repeat this step with the medium starfish, so that you have two base shapes filled with the 11 ovoid petals.

4 Pick up the medium starfish/ovoid petal shape with the tweezers and use the toothpick to apply a small amount of glue to the bottom of it. Set it in place on top of the medium snowflake/ovoid petal shape, then press down in the center of the piece with the tip of the tweezers to secure it.

5 Place the black medium delicate snowflakes on the art gum eraser and use the small ball stylus to cup them. Then use the tweezers to pick up one of the snowflakes and apply glue to the bottom of it with the toothpick. Set the snowflake in

place in the center of the flower. Repeat this step with the second medium delicate snowflake.

6 Use the small scissors to cut the rays of the small black sun in half. Then place the shape on the art gum eraser and use the small ball stylus to cup it. Pick up the sun with the tweezers, use the toothpick to apply glue to the bottom of it, and set it in place in the center of the last black medium delicate snowflake.

7 Place the small black snowflake on the art gum eraser and use the small ball stylus to cup it. Then pick up the snowflake with the tweezers and use the toothpick to apply a small amount of glue to the bottom of it. Place the snowflake in the center of the small sun.

8 Place one of the medium ivy leaves on the rubber mat, right-side down, then use the small ball stylus to create a stem line down the center of the leaf. Turn the shape right-side up and add a few vein lines using the small ball stylus. Shape as desired (refer to page 15 for shaping techniques). Repeat this step with each of the leaves. Set the flower in place on your project and tuck the leaves under it to finish.

TOPPERS

Choose a beautiful box, and add a single paper blossom or a bouquet to the top. You can use a pre-colored box or a papier-mâché box painted with acrylic paints. There's no limitation to the kind of container you can embellish—try adding paper flowers to a bag of baked goods or a jar of jam.

ASTER

The name aster comes from the Latin word astrum, which means star. The Greeks believed that asters could repel snakes and serve as an antidote to their venom. The delicate daisy petals of this pretty flower make it a perfect addition to any autumn paper bouquet.

Level of difficulty: 🌸 🌸

Punches for flower and quantity needed
3 large sunflowers for flower [a]
3 mini suns for stamen [b]

Punch for leaves and quantity needed
3–4 medium chestnut leaves [c]

a   b   c

Tools and Supplies
Basic Tool Kit (page 11)
Recommended cardstock colors:
White, pink, magenta, or periwinkle blue for sunflower
Bright yellow for mini sun
Yellow and green for chestnut leaves

ASTER

To make the flower

1 Use the small scissors to cut the petals of all of the sunflowers into thirds.

2 Place the three sunflowers right-side up on the rubber mat and use the large ball stylus to cup each one, following the instructions for cupping on page 15. Set one of the sunflowers on the rubber mat to serve as the base. Then use the toothpick to apply a small amount of glue to the bottom of the remaining sunflower shapes and layer them on top of the base sunflower, one at a time. Use the tip of the tweezers to press down on the center of the piece as you set each layer.

3 Place two of the mini suns on the art gum eraser. Use the small stylus to cup each one, then add a small amount of glue to the bottom of each sun. Place each sun, one at a time, in the center of the flower.

4 Use the small scissors to cut about two-thirds of the way through the center of the mini sun. Grasp one side of the sun with the tweezers and roll the shape into a cone. Apply a small amount of glue to the end of the sun to secure it. Hold the rolled-up sun with the tweezers to set it, then place it in the center of the last sun.

(**Tip:** Use a soft toothbrush to fluff out the petals after the glue has dried completely.)

5 Place one of the medium chestnut leaves right-side down on the rubber mat. Use the small ball stylus to create a stem line down the center of the leaf. Shape as desired (refer to page 15 for shaping techniques). Repeat with the remaining leaves. Set the flower in place on your project and glue the leaves under it to finish.

AZALEA

This flowering shrub is one of the showiest plants in bloom during the spring season. It's part of the rhododendron group and a popular, colorful addition to the garden.

Level of difficulty:

Punches for flower and quantity needed
- 1 large blossom for flower [a]
- 1 medium blossom for flower [b]
- 1 medium lily for flower [c]
- 1 small cosmo for stamen [d]

Punch for leaves and quantity needed
- 2–3 small birch leaves [e]

a   b   c   d   e

Tools and Supplies
- Basic Tool Kit (page 11)
- Recommended cardstock colors:
  - White, lavender, peach, or various shades of pink for large blossom, medium blossom, and lily
  - Pale yellow for stamen
  - Dark green for birch leaves
- Pigment marker pen in brownish red

To make the flower

1 Use the small scissors to make cuts of approximately ¼ inch (6 mm) in between the petals of both blossoms and the lily shape.

2 Place the blossoms and the lily shape wrong-side down on the rubber mat and use the rounded end of the molding tool or large ball stylus to shape them (refer to page 15 for shaping techniques). Then turn the shapes right-side up and use the medium ball stylus to stir the shapes, following the instructions for stirring on page 17.

3 Use the pigment ink marker to tip the ends of the cosmo on both sides. Then use the small scissors to cut each petal of the cosmo in half and place it on the art gum eraser. Use the small stylus to cup the cosmo shape, following the instructions for cupping on page 15. Then use the toothpick to add a small amount of glue to the center of the shape and close it up. Pinch the shape closed at the base for about one minute to allow the glue to set.

4 Use the toothpick to add a small amount of glue to the bottom of the medium blossom and place it on top of the large blossom, pressing down lightly in the center of the piece with the end of the tweezers. Repeat this gluing and layering technique to place the medium lily shape on top of the medium blossom.

5 Use the tweezers to pick up the closed cosmo, dip the bottom end of the shape into the glue, and place it in the center of the lily shape.

6 To make the leaves, refer to step 5 of the Aster project on page 31.

BACHELOR'S BUTTON

This blossom's nickname—cornflower—was inspired by the fact that the flowers grow wild in the cornfields of southern Europe. When Napoleon drove Queen Louise of Prussia out of Berlin, she hid her children in a cornfield and kept them quiet by making wreaths of the flowers. The flower is the emblem of national unity in Germany.

Level of difficulty: 🌸

Punches for flower and quantity needed
   6 medium cosmos for flower [a]
   2 small cosmos for flower [b]
   1 mini snowflake for stamen [c]
   1 small kikyou for base of flower [d]

Punch for leaves and quantity needed
   2–3 medium dusty miller leaves [e]

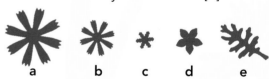

a　　b　　c　　d　　e

Tools and Supplies
   Basic Tool Kit (page 11)
   Recommended cardstock colors:
      Sky blue, periwinkle blue, pink, or pale yellow for medium cosmos
      A darker shade for small cosmos
      Black for mini snowflake
      Bright green for kikyou
      Light green for leaves

To make the flower

1 Use the small scissors to cut the petals of all of the medium and small cosmos in half. Use your fingers to fluff open the petals.

2 Place the medium cosmos on the rubber mat and use the medium ball stylus to cup them, following the instructions for cupping on page 15.

3 Place one of the medium cosmos on the rubber mat to serve as a base. Pick up another medium cosmos with the tweezers, then use the toothpick to apply a small amount of the glue to the bottom of the shape. Place this cosmos on top of the base cosmos. Repeat this step with the next four medium cosmos. As you layer the shapes, offset the petals.

4 Place the two small cosmos on the art gum eraser and use the small ball stylus to cup them.

5 Pick up one of the small cosmos with the tweezers, then use the toothpick to apply a small amount of glue to the bottom of the shape. Set the shape on top of the layered medium cosmos, pressing down slightly in the middle of the piece with the tip of the tweezers. Repeat this gluing and layering technique with the other small cosmos.

6 Place the mini snowflake on the art gum eraser and use the small ball stylus to cup it. Then grasp the snowflake with the tweezers and use the toothpick to apply a small amount of glue to the bottom of it. Set the snowflake in place on top of the last small cosmos. Press down with the tip of the tweezers to set the shape.

7 Place the small kikyou base right-side down on the art gum eraser, then use the small ball stylus to cup it. Use the toothpick to apply a small amount of glue to the inside of the kikyou and attach it to the bottom cosmos flower. This will create a base for attaching the flower to your project.

8 Allow the flower to dry for 10 to 15 minutes, then fluff the petals again.

9 To make the leaves, refer to step 5 of the Aster project on page 31.

BEGONIA

The begonia was named after Michel Bégon, governor of Santo Domingo and French Canada in the fifteenth century. Begonias are selected for container gardens. Try creating some of the variegated kind in paper, using chalks to shade the petals.

Level of difficulty: ✿ ✿

Punches for flower and quantity needed

20 super giant begonia petals for flower [a]
(For punch key and individual pieces used, see page 124.)

1 medium starfish for base of flower [b]

Punch for leaves and quantity needed

3–4 large geranium leaves [c]

a   b   c

Tools and Supplies

Basic Tool Kit (page 11)
Recommended cardstock:
  White, pink, red, yellow or orange for begonias
  Medium green for medium starfish
  Olive, medium, or dark green for leaves
Chalk in colors to complement cardstock

BEGONIA

To make the flower

1 Punch the super giant begonia petals five times in your chosen cardstock color to produce a total of 25 petals. You won't need the very largest petals, so set those shapes aside.

2 Place all of the begonia petals on the rubber mat and use the rounded end of the molding tool or large ball stylus to shape them (refer to page 15 for shaping techniques). Then pinch and bend each of the petals, following the instructions for pinching and bending on page 16.

3 If you are creating a variegated begonia, use the chalk to shade the outer edges of each of the petals.

4 Place the starfish shape on the rubber mat and cup it, following the instructions for cupping on page 15.

5 Pick out the five largest begonia petals, then dip the small end of each of them into the glue and place each one on a projection of the starfish shape. Continue this process until you have set the five largest petals on the starfish shape.

6 Pick out the next largest size of begonia petals and dip the small end of each of them into the glue. Then place each of the five petals just inside the first row of petals, with the small end of each piece pointing toward the center of the flower. Make sure this second row of petals is offset from the first. As you add the petals, make sure you leave the middle of the flower open, so there will be room to add the final center petals.

7 Pick out three or four of the smaller petals and dip the small end of each of them into the glue. Then set them upright in the center of the flower. Use the tweezers to roll up one or two of the smallest petals, dip the ends of the petals into the glue and place them in the center of the flower.

8 Place one of the leaves right-side down on the rubber mat, then use the small ball stylus to create three or four lines down the length of the leaf. Shape the leaf as desired (refer to page 15 for shaping techniques). Repeat this step with two or three more leaves. Set the flower in place on your project and tuck the leaves under it to finish.

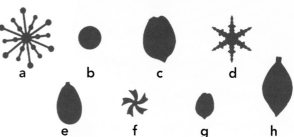

Camellia

Cherished for its classic beauty, the camellia is known and loved throughout the world. More than 100 different species of the flower are known to exist. With petals in shades of pink, yellow, and red, this evergreen shrub is a beautiful addition to any project.

Level of difficulty: ✿ ✿

Punches for flower and quantity needed

1 large delicate snowflake for base of flower [a]

1 small circle for base of flower [b]

16 large ovoid petals for flower [c]

2 medium snowflakes for base of flower [d]

6 super giant moth orchids for flower [e]
   (For punch key and individual pieces used, see page 124.)

1 small pinwheel for base of flower [f]

7–8 small ovoid petals for flower [g]

Punch for leaves and quantity needed

3–4 super giant lilacs/daphne [h]
   (For punch key and individual pieces used, see page 124.)

a   b   c   d

e   f   g   h

Tools and Supplies

Basic Tool Kit (page 11)

Recommended cardstock:

Dark green for snowflakes, circle, pinwheel, and lilacs

White, carmine, red, or various shades of pink for moth orchids and ovoid petals

Chalk for shading (optional)

Gel pen in charcoal

To make the flower

1 Place the large delicate snowflake on the rubber mat and use the large ball stylus to cup it, following the instructions for cupping on page 15. Place the small circle on the mat, then use the round end of the molding tool to shape it (refer to page 15 for shaping techniques). Use the toothpick to apply a small amount of the glue to the bottom of the snowflake, then attach it to the circle. This will stabilize the snowflake.

2 Place the large ovoid petals on the rubber mat and use the rounded end of the molding tool or the large ball stylus to shape them. Then pinch and bend each of the large ovoid petals, following the instructions for pinching and bending on page 16. Optional: Shade the base of all the petals with chalk, referring to page 14 for information on shading.

3 With the small ball stylus, hold the snowflake/circle shape securely on the rubber mat while you use the tweezers to pick up one of the large ovoid petals at its tip. Dip the stem of the petal into the glue and place it on the snowflake base, about ¼ inch (6 mm) in from the outer edge. Attach 10 of the large ovoid petals to the snowflake base, spacing them out evenly.

4 Place the two medium snowflakes on the rubber mat and cup them with the large ball stylus. Grasp one of the medium snowflakes with the tweezers, then use the toothpick to apply a small amount of the glue to the bottom of the snowflake. Place the medium snowflake in the center of the large snowflake. Then repeat step 3 with six more of the large ovoid petals, attaching them to the projections of the medium snowflake.

Place the second medium snowflake in the center of the previous medium snowflake.

5 Punch the super giant moth orchid six times to produce 30 pieces. You will only use the six balloon-shaped petals. Place the six balloon-shaped petals on the rubber mat and use the round end of the molding tool or large ball stylus to shape them. Pinch and bend each of the petals. Then hold the flower securely with the small ball stylus while you use the tweezers to pick up one of the petals. Dip the stem of the petal into the glue and place it on one of the medium snowflake projections. Repeat this step with the remaining five petals.

6 Place the pinwheel on the rubber mat and cup it. Then grasp the pinwheel with the tweezers, use the toothpick to add a dab of glue to the bottom of it and place it on top of the snowflake.

7 Place the small ovoid petals on the rubber mat and use the large ball stylus to shape each of them. Then pinch and bend each of the petals. Use the small ball stylus to hold the flower securely, then grasp one of the petals with the tweezers, dip the stem into the glue, and place the petal on one of the pinwheel's projections. Use the additional small ovoid petals to fill in as needed.

8 Punch the super giant lilacs/daphne four times to produce four leaves. Place one of the leaves on the rubber mat and use the gel pen to draw a stem line down the center. Turn the leaf right-side down and use the small ball stylus to add a stem line down the center of the leaf. Shape as desired (refer to page 15 for shaping techniques). Repeat this step to make a total of three to four leaves. Then set the flower in place on your project and tuck the leaves under it to finish.

CARNATION

Carnations are sometimes referred to as pinks. Widely known as a favorite boutonnière or corsage flower, the perennial is often worn on Mother's Day. Create one from paper, and you'll have a special blossom all your own.

Level of difficulty: ✿ ✿

Punches for flower and quantity needed

1 medium sun for base [a]

20–25 super giant begonia petals [b]

(For punch key and individual pieces used, see page 124.)

Punch for leaves and quantity needed

3–4 mega elongated leaves [c]

(For punch key and individual pieces used, see page 124.)

a   b   c

Tools and Supplies

Basic Tool Kit (page 11)

Recommended cardstock:

    Medium green for medium sun and elongated leaves

    Various shades of pink, white, crimson, purple, or yellow for begonia petals

Paper shaping scissors with a pinking edge

Pigment marker or pearlescent watercolor in a color to complement cardstock

Brush

To make the flower

1 Punch the super giant begonia petals five to six times to produce a total of 25–30 petals. You won't need the largest petals, so set those shapes aside.

2 Use the small scissors to cut approximately two-thirds of the way through the center of the medium sun. Then grasp one side of the sun with the tweezers and roll it into a cone, adding a small amount of glue with the toothpick to the other end before closing the shape. Use the tweezers to hold the shape for a few minutes until it's set.

3 Use the pinking scissors to trim the outer edge of all of the begonia petals. Then place the petals on the rubber mat and use the round end of the molding tool or the large ball stylus to shape them (refer to page 15 for shaping techniques). Optional: Add color to the tips of the petals with the pigment marker or the watercolor paint.

4 Pinch and bend each of the petals, following the instructions for pinching and bending on page 16.

5 Use the tweezers to pick up one of the larger petals and dip the stem of it into the glue. Place the petal in the cone shape, then add the other petals, overlapping them slightly as you complete the first round.

6 Continue adding petals, graduated in size and overlapping slightly, as you did in the previous step.

7 Use the tweezers to roll up one or two of the smallest petals, then dip the ends of each petal into the glue and add them to the center of the flower.

8 Punch the mega elongated leaves two times to produce a total of six leaves. Add three or four of the largest elongated leaves to the carnation by referring to step 5 of the Aster project on page 31.

CHERRY BLOSSOM

This delicate tree is Japan's unofficial national flower. Most cherry blossom trees bloom for just a couple of days during the spring. The Japanese people have viewing parties called Hanami under the trees when they're in bloom.

Level of difficulty: ✿ ✿

Punches for flower and quantity needed
2 medium blossoms for flower [a]
1 large splatt for flower [b]
1 small cosmo for stamen [c]
1 mini sun for base of stamen [d]

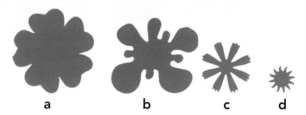

a   b   c   d

Tools and Supplies
Basic Tool Kit (page 11)
Recommended cardstock:
  Various shades of pink for medium blossoms and splatt
  Pale yellow for small cosmo
  Pinkish purple for mini sun
Pigment marker in pinkish purple

For branch (optional):
Wire cutters
Paper-covered craft wire
Brown floral tape

To make the flower

1 Use the small scissors to make cuts that are approximately ¼ inch (6 mm) between the petals of both of the medium blossoms. Do the same in several places on the splatt.

2 Place the blossoms and the splatt wrong-side down on the rubber mat and use the half-rounded end of the molding tool or the large ball stylus to shape each of them (refer to page 15 for shaping techniques). Turn the shapes right-side up and use the medium ball stylus to stir them, following the instructions for stirring on page 17.

3 Use the tweezers to pick up one of the blossoms and lightly dip the bottom center portion of it into the glue. Place this blossom on top of the other blossom on the rubber mat, then press down in the center of the blossoms with the point of the tweezers to secure. Repeat this process with the splatt, layering it on top of the blossoms and pressing down in the center of the piece with the tweezers.

4 Use the pigment marker to tip the ends of the cosmo on both sides. Then use the small scissors to cut each petal of the cosmo in half.

5 Place the cosmo on the art gum eraser and use the small ball stylus to cup it, following the instructions for cupping on page 15. Use the toothpick to add a small amount of glue to the center of the cosmo, then pinch the shape closed at the base for about one minute so the glue can set.

6 Place the mini sun on the art gum eraser and use the small stylus to cup it. Use the tweezers to pick up the sun, then add a small amount of glue to the bottom of it with the toothpick. Place the shape in the center of the flower. Then use the tweezers to pick up the cosmo and place it on top of the sun.

To add a branch (optional)

No leaves are needed for this project, because cherry blossoms appear before leaves can develop. However, you may want to create a branch to show the blossoms off.

7 Use the wire cutters to cut the desired length of branch from the craft wire. Then cut two more lengths that are shorter than the first to create divisions on the branch.

8 Use the brown floral tape to wrap the branch at the "tree" end, pulling snuggly as you wrap. Add one of the division pieces, then continue wrapping to incorporate it into the main branch. When you reach the end of the branch, cut the floral tape so that it's slightly longer than the branch and continue to wrap to form a tapered look. Add the second division piece, making sure you cover the entire branch with the floral tape. Then dip the flowers into the glue and attach them to the branch as desired.

CHRYSANTHEMUM

In Japanese art, the chrysanthemum represents longevity and happiness. Some species of the flower resemble daisies, while others have a pompom-like appearance. Both varieties will make beautiful paper bouquets.

Level of difficulty: ✿ ✿

Punches for pompom version and quantity needed
3 large daisies for flower [a]
3 silhouette daisies for flower [b]
4 small daisies for flower [c]

Punches for daisy version and quantity needed
16 small ovoid petals for flower [d]
2 large daisies for flower [a]
1 silhouette daisy for flower [b]
1 small blossom for stamen [e]

Punch for leaves and quantity needed
3–4 large oak leaves [f]

a   b   c   d   e   f

Tools and Supplies
Basic Tool Kit (page 11)
Recommended cardstock:
  For pompom version: Yellow, rust, white, or various shades of pink for all daisies
  For daisy version: White, red, purple, or various shades of pink for daisies and petals
  Bright yellow for small blossom
Medium or olive green for oak leaves
Chalk in shades that contrast with cardstock (optional)

To make the pompom version

1 Optional: Use the chalk to add shading to all of the daisy shapes.

2 Pinch the petals of the large daisies and the silhouette daisies, following the instructions for pinching on page 16. Then place the shapes on the rubber mat and cup them, following the instructions for cupping on page 15. Set the pieces aside.

3 Place three of the four small daisies right-side down on the rubber mat and shape them with the large ball stylus (refer to page 15 for shaping techniques). Then turn the daisies right-side up and place three of them on the art gum eraser. Use the small ball stylus to cup both of the daisies.

4 Use the small scissors to cut two-thirds of the way into the center of the fourth small daisy. Then use the tweezers to grasp one side of the daisy and roll it up, adding a small amount of glue with the toothpick to secure the rolled shape. Hold the piece for a few seconds to set it.

5 Place one of the large daisies on the rubber mat. Use the tooth-pick to apply a small amount of glue to another one of the large daisies and set it on top of the first, making sure the petals are offset. Repeat this step to add the third large daisy, then use the tip of the tweezers to press down in the center of the piece to secure it.

6 Repeat the gluing and layering technique from step 5 with the three silhouette daisies, then the two small daisies. Then pick up the small rolled daisy, dip the bottom of it into the glue, and set it in the center of the flower.

To make the daisy version

1 Optional: Use the chalk to add shading to the ovoid petals.

2 Place the two large daisies on the rubber mat and use the round end of the molding tool or the large ball stylus to cup them. Set the pieces aside.

3 Place the ovoid petals on the rubber mat and use the large ball stylus to shape them. Then pinch and bend each of the petals, following the instructions for pinching and bending on page 16.

4 Pick up one of the petals with the tweezers, dip the pinched end of it into the glue, and attach it to one of the petals on a large daisy. Repeat this step so that you have two large daisies with ovoid petals attached to each of their petals.

5 Use the tweezers to pinch each petal of the silhouette flower, then place the flower on the rubber mat and cup it.

6 Place one of the large daisies with ovoid petals on the rubber mat. Use the toothpick to apply a small amount of the glue to the second daisy with ovoid petals and layer it on top of the first, offsetting the petals.

7 Use the toothpick to apply a small amount of glue to the silhouette flower and layer it on top of the second daisy. Press down on the piece with the tip of the tweezers to secure.

8 Place the small blossom right-side down on the rubber mat and use the medium ball stylus to shape it. Then stir it, following the instructions for stirring on page 17. Use the toothpick to apply glue to the center of the silhouette flower. Then pick up the small blossom with the tweezers and set it right-side up in the center of the silhouette flower.

9 To make leaves for each type of chrysanthemum, refer to step 5 of the Aster project on page 31.

BABY OR WEDDING ALBUMS

Paper flowers add something extra to any memory or photo album. If you're decorating a baby album, add paper flowers that depict the season in which the birth takes place as a special remembrance. If you're decorating a wedding album, match your paper flowers to the bridal bouquet. Use the flowers to encircle the photo on the cover of the album.

CLEMATIS

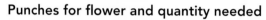

This showy flower has numerous fluffy seed heads and blooms from early spring to midsummer. The clematis is also known as the Virgin's bower, because of the German legend that Mary and Jesus sheltered under a clematis during their flight from Egypt. Since the petal-like sepals of the flower vary, I use two different bases when creating my favorite variety.

Level of difficulty: ✿ ✿

Punches for flower and quantity needed
8 mega giant dahlia petals [a]
  (For punch key and individual pieces used, see page 124.)
1 large daisy for base of 8-petal flower [b]
1 medium snowflake for base of 6-petal flower [c]
2–3 medium sparkles for stamen [d]
2–3 small sparkles for stamen [e]
2–3 small suns for stamen [f]
1 mini sun for stamen [g]

Punch for leaves and quantity needed
2–3 super giant birch leaves [h]

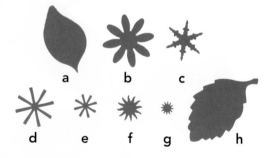

Tools and Supplies
Basic Tool Kit (page 11)
Recommended cardstock:
   White, blue, cream, or various shades of pink or purple for petals
   Medium green for large daisy, medium snowflake, and birch leaves
   Pale yellow, light green, or brownish red for sparkles
   Pale yellow for suns
Deckle scissors
Chalk in colors to replicate shading on petals
Pigment marker in brownish red

To make the flower

1 Place the large daisy (for the eight-petaled flower) or the medium snowflake (for the six-petaled flower) on the rubber mat and cup it, following the instructions for cupping on page 15.

2 Punch the mega giant dahlia petals eight times to produce a total of 40 pieces. You will only use the eight largest petals. Use the deckle scissors to add detail to the sides of the dahlia petals. Then use the chalk to shade the petals appropriately.

3 Place the dahlia petals wrong-side up on the rubber mat and use the round end of the molding tool or the large ball stylus to shape them (refer to page 15 for shaping techniques). Then turn the petals right-side up and repeat the shaping process. (The petals will have a more natural, wrinkly look to them, thanks to this double shaping.) Pinch and bend each of the petals, following the instructions for pinching and bending on page 16.

4 Use the small ball stylus to hold the large daisy or medium snowflake securely on the rubber mat while you use the tweezers to pick up a dahlia petal. Dip the pinched end of the petal into the glue, then place the petal on a projection of the daisy or the snowflake. Repeat with each of the dahlia petals.

5 To make the seed head, use the pigment marker to tip the ends of the sparkles and the small suns. Then use the scissors to cut the projections of each sparkle and the rays of each small sun in half.

6 Place the small and medium sparkles and the small suns on the art gum eraser and cup all of them. Then use the toothpick to apply a small amount of glue to each sparkle and sun, and add the pieces to the center of the flower following this sequence: 2 to 3 medium sparkles, 2 to 3 small sparkles, 2 to 3 small suns.

7 Place the mini sun on the art gum eraser and cup it. Hold the sun with the tweezers, then use the toothpick to apply a small amount of glue to the bottom. Set the mini sun in the center of the seed head.

8 Place one of the super giant birch leaves right-side down on the rubber mat. Use the small ball stylus to create a stem line down the center of the leaf. Turn the leaf right-side up and add vein lines from the stem line to the outer edge with the small ball stylus. Shape as desired (refer to page 15 for shaping techniques). Repeat this step with each of the leaves. Then set the flower in place on your project and tuck the leaves under it to finish.

COREOPSIS

Included in the daisy family, this perennial is native to Mexico. The coreopsis was used by Native Americans to create orange and red dyes. In a paper garden, the contrasting centers of the flower add interest to other blossom combinations.

Level of difficulty: ✺

Punches for flower and quantity needed
1 large daisy for flower [a]
3 small suns for the stamen [b]

Punch for leaves and quantity needed
2–3 medium dusty miller leaves [c]

a   b   c

Tools and Supplies
Basic Tool Kit (page 11)
Recommended cardstock:
Light yellow for daisy
Bright yellow for small suns
Bright to medium green for leaves
Pigment ink pen in brownish red or maroon

COREOPSIS

To make the flower

1 Pinch each of the petals on the large daisy, following the instructions for pinching on page 16. Then place the daisy on the rubber mat and use the large ball stylus to cup it, following the instructions for cupping on page 15.

2 Use the pigment ink pen to tip the ends of the three small suns on the front and back.

3 Use the small scissors to cut the rays of each of the suns in half. Then place two of the suns on the rubber mat and use the small ball stylus to stir them, following the instructions for stirring on page 17. Use the toothpick to apply small dabs of glue to the bottom of each of the suns. Then place the suns, one at a time, in the center of the daisy.

4 Use the scissors to cut ⅔ of the way through the center of the third sun. Then use the tweezers to grasp one side of the sun and roll it into a cone. Use the toothpick to apply a small dab of glue to one end of the cone, then close the shape completely. Hold the cone for a few seconds to let the glue set. Then pick up the cone-shaped sun, dip the bottom of it into the glue and place it in the center of the flower.

5 To make the leaves, refer to step 5 of the Aster project on page 31.

COSMOS

The name of this flower comes from the Greek word *kosmos,* which means *beautiful. This striking annual can be found in most gardens from summer to mid-autumn. Create a cluster of cosmos and add it to a tag or gift box—it'll dress up any package.*

Level of difficulty:

Punches for flower and quantity needed
4 large hearts for flower [a]
1 medium cosmos for base of flower [b]
4 small suns for stamen [c]
1 mini sun for stamen [d]

Punch for leaves and quantity needed
3–4 medium dusty miller leaves [e]

a   b   c   d   e

Tools and Supplies
Basic Tool Kit (page 11)
Recommended cardstock:
  White, purple, red, or various shades of pink for the large hearts
  Bright green for medium cosmos and leaves
  Bright yellow for the small suns and mini sun
Deckle scissors
Chalk for shading (optional)

COSMOS

To make the flower

1 Use the small scissors to cut each of the hearts in half. Then use the deckle scissors to add detail to the tops of the petals.

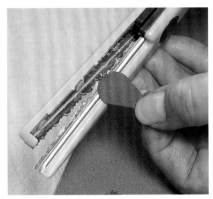

2 Place the medium cosmos shape on the rubber mat and cup it, following the instructions for cupping on page 15.

3 Place the heart halves on the rubber mat and use the round end of the molding tool or large ball stylus to shape the pieces into petals (refer to page 15 for shaping techniques). Then pinch and bend each of the petals, following the instructions for pinching and bending on page 16.

4 Use the small ball stylus to hold the cosmos shape securely on the rubber mat. Hold the petals with the tweezers and dip the pinched end into the glue. Place one petal on each of the projections of the cosmos shape.

5 Use the scissors to cut each ray of the small suns and the mini sun in half. Then use the tweezers to grasp one of the rays on the small sun and roll it towards the center. Do this for each ray on the four small suns and the mini sun. Place the small suns on the rubber mat and use the medium ball stylus to stir them, following the instructions for stirring on page 17. Then place the mini sun on the art gum eraser and cup it.

6 Use the toothpick to apply a small amount of glue to the bottom of the small suns and the mini sun, and place them in the center of the flower. Press down on the center of the flower with the tip of the tweezers to secure the suns.

7 To make the leaves, refer to step 5 of the Aster project on page 31.

DAFFODIL

According to Greek mythology, Narcissus was a young boy who fell in love with his own reflection when he saw it in a pond. Transfixed by his reflection, he eventually wasted away and became a flower. Daffodils—sometimes called jonquils—fall under the genus Narcissus. The numerous colors of this special flower make it a favorite for early spring.

Level of difficulty: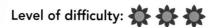

Punches for flower and quantity needed

1 large scallop oval for flower crown [a]

6 super giant cymbidium orchids for petals [b]
(For punch key and individual pieces used, see page 124.)

1 large snowflake for base of flower [c]

1 medium pollen for stamen [d]

Punch for leaves and quantity needed

2–3 mega elongated leaves [e]
(For punch key and individual pieces used, see page 124.)

a   b   c   d   e

Tools and Supplies

Basic Tool Kit (page 11)

Recommended cardstock:

  White, yellow, peach, or pink for large oval

  White or yellow for petals from orchids

  Pale yellow for medium pollen

  Medium green for large snowflake and elongated leaves

Small drinking glass with at least a 2½-inch (6.4 cm) opening

#2 pencil

Deckle scissors

Pigment ink marker in bright green

To make the flower

1 To make the crown of the flower, turn the glass upside down and place it on top of the large scallop oval. Approximately 1 inch (2.5 cm) of the oval should be visible above the glass. Use the pencil to trace the arc of the glass onto the oval. Then use the small scissors to cut along the penciled line and to trim the sides of the oval as shown. Discard the bottom piece of the oval.

2 Use the deckle scissors to edge the top scallops on the remaining oval piece. This will produce a more natural-looking petal. Use the small scissors to make ¼-inch (6 mm) cuts between each scallop, then trim the sides to form tabs for gluing the crown together.

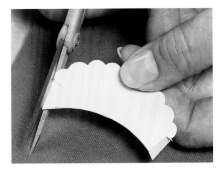

3 Place the trimmed oval scallop on the rubber mat and use the concave end of the molding tool to shape it (refer to page 15 for shaping techniques). The scallop will begin to roll up. Use the toothpick to apply a small amount of glue to one side of the scallop, then use the tweezers to grasp the other side and bring it to the glued side. Use the tweezers to hold the rolled shape for one to two minutes until the glue sets. Then use the tweezers to bend down the scallops. Set the piece aside until needed.

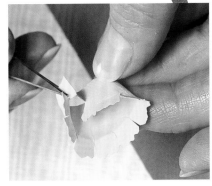

4 Punch the super giant cymbidium orchid six times to produce 30 pieces. You will only use six of the petals. Place the petals on the rubber mat and use the round end of the molding tool to shape each petal. Pinch and bend each of the petals, following the instructions for pinching and bending on page 16.

5 Place the snowflake on the rubber mat, then use the medium ball stylus to cup it, following the instructions for cupping on page 15.

6 Use the small ball stylus to hold the snowflake in place on the rubber mat, then use your free hand to pick up one of the petals with the tweezers and dip the stem of the petal into the glue. Adhere the petal to one of the projections on the snowflake. Repeat with all of the petals, making sure the center of the snowflake remains open so you can add the crown.

7 Use the tweezers to pick up the crown by its top, then dip the bottom of it into the glue. Attach it to the center of the flower, pressing down slightly with the tweezers.

8 Use the bright green pen to tip the ends of the medium pollen on both sides. Then use the tweezers to grasp one end of the shape and roll it up, leaving a small section unrolled. Apply glue to this section with a toothpick, then close up the roll.

9 Use the tweezers to pick up the closed pollen shape, dip the bottom of it into the glue and set it inside the crown of the daffodil.

10 Punch the mega elongated leaves once to produce three leaves. Add two or three leaves to the daffodil by referring to step 5 of the Aster project on page 31.

DOGWOOD

Four simple oval petals that form opposite one another make this flowering tree easily identifiable in the spring. To create lifelike bracts for the blossom, add a touch of glitter glue to the stamen as you make your dogwood.

Level of difficulty: 🌸 🌸

Punches for flower and quantity needed

4 super giant moth orchids for flower [a]
(For punch key and individual pieces used, see page 124.)

1 small jack for base of flower [b]

1 small cross for base of flower [c]

2 small suns for stamen [d]

1 mini sun for stamen [e]

Punch for leaves and quantity needed

4 medium impatiens leaves [f]

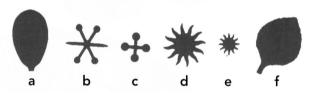

a   b   c   d   e   f

Tools and Supplies

Basic Tool Kit (page 11)

Recommended cardstock colors:

   Creamy white or pink for petals from moth orchids

   Medium green for small jack, small cross, and leaves

   Bright green for small suns and mini sun

Round hand punch, 1/8 inch (3 mm)

Brownish red pigment marker pen

Chalk in medium pink

Colored pencil in medium pink

Lime green glitter glue (optional)

To make the flower

1 Punch the super giant moth orchid four times to produce a total of 20 pieces. You will only use the four balloon-shaped petals. Use the hand punch to make a small notch in the top of one of the balloon-shaped petals from the moth orchid punch. Then use the pigment marker to shade the notch. Repeat this step with the three remaining petals.

If you're creating a pink dogwood blossom, shade the base of each petal with the chalk and use the colored pencil to add vein lines.

2 Place the small jack and the cross on the rubber mat, then use the small ball stylus to cup the shapes, following the instructions for cupping on page 15. Use the toothpick to add a small amount of the glue to the bottom of the jack, then place it on top of the cross. This will create a stable base for supporting the petals of the flower.

3 Place the four petals on the rubber mat and use the rounded end of the molding tool or the large ball stylus to shape them (refer to page 15 for shaping techniques). Then pinch and bend each of the petals, following the instructions for pinching and bending on page 16.

4 Use the small ball stylus to hold the jack/cross shape securely on the rubber mat, then use your free hand to pick up one of the petals with the tweezers. Dip the stem of the petal into the glue and place it on the base, leaving about ⅛ inch (3 mm) of space in the center so that you can add the stamen. Repeat this step with the other three petals.

5 Use the small scissors to cut through the rays of the two small suns, cutting a little further into the center every other time. Use the tweezers to roll the snipped rays toward the center of each of the suns. Then place the suns back on the rubber mat and use the medium ball stylus to stir the shapes, following the instructions for stirring on page 17.

6 Use the small scissors to cut two-thirds of the way into the center of the mini sun shape. Grasp one side of the sun with the tweezers and roll it counterclockwise into a cone shape, leaving a small area unrolled for gluing. Use the toothpick to dab a small amount of glue on the unrolled area, then finish rolling the sun up. Hold the rolled shape for one to two minutes with your thumb and index finger to set the glue.

7 Pick up one of the medium suns, dip the bottom lightly in the glue and place it in the center of the four petals. Repeat this step with the second medium sun, placing it in the center of the first medium sun. Then pick up the mini sun with the tweezers, use the toothpick to dab a small amount of glue on the bottom of it, and attach it to the center of the medium suns.

8 Optional: Add further detail to the center of the blossom by adding tiny drops of the lime green glitter glue to replicate the bracts of a dogwood.

9 Place one of the leaves right-side down on the rubber mat. Use the small ball stylus to make a stem line down the center of the leaf, then turn the leaf over and add vein lines from the stem line to the outside edge. Shape the leaf as desired (refer to page 15 for shaping techniques). Repeat this step with each leaf. Set the flower in place on your project, then tuck the leaves under it to finish.

ECHINACEA

The echinacea is part of the daisy family and used extensively in herbal remedies because it is thought to enhance the immune system. Because the echinacea is also known as the coneflower, I re-created the center of the flower in paper using color combinations to accentuate the cone characteristic.

Level of difficulty:

Punches for flower and quantity needed
3 super giant daisies for flower [a]
8 medium suns for stamen [b]

Punch for leaves and quantity needed
2–3 large oak leaves [c]

a   b   c

Tools and Supplies
Basic Tool Kit (page 11)
Recommended cardstock:
  Bright yellow, white, or various shades of pink for giant daisies
  Brown, yellow, yellowish green, and orange for medium suns (use a combination of two colors when punching suns)
  Bright to medium green for leaves

To make the flower

1 Pinch each of the petals on the super giant daisies, following the instructions for pinching on page 16. Then place the daisies on the rubber mat and use the rounded end of the molding tool to cup each of the flowers, following the instructions for cupping on page 15.

2 Place one of the super giant daisies on the rubber mat as a base. Grasp another super giant daisy with the tweezers, then use the toothpick to apply a small amount of glue to the bottom of the daisy. Set the shape on top of the base daisy, making sure the petals are offset. Repeat this step with the third daisy, then use the tip of the tweezers to press down on the center of the piece to secure all of the layers.

3 Use the small scissors to cut the rays on seven of the medium suns in half. Then use the tweezers to grasp the cut rays and roll them toward the center.

4 Place the medium suns on the rubber mat and use the medium ball stylus to stir them, following the instructions for stirring on page 17. Pick up one of the suns with the tweezers and use the toothpick to apply a small amount of glue to the bottom of it. Then set the sun in the center of the flower. Repeat with six more suns, alternating colors of brown and orange, brown and yellow, or yellow and green for the suns.

5 Use the small scissors to cut the last medium sun two-thirds of the way through the center. Grasp one side of the sun with the tweezers and roll it up, then use the toothpick to apply a small amount of glue to the open side. Roll the shape up and hold it for a few seconds, then use the tweezers to dip the bottom of the roll into the glue. Place it in the center of the last medium sun to complete the center of the flower.

6 To add the leaves, refer to step 5 of the Aster project on page 31.

FORSYTHIA

This bright, starry flower is a cheerful sign of spring. In fact, the flowers appear on the branches of this shrub before the season's first leaves.

Level of difficulty: ✱

Punches for flower and quantity needed
30–40 mini flowers for flower [a]

Punch for leaves and quantity needed
3–4 small birch leaves per stem [b]

a   b

Tools and Supplies
Basic Tool Kit (page 11)
Recommended cardstock colors:
    Various shades of yellow for mini flowers
    Bright green for birch leaves
Craft knife
3-inch (7.6 cm) polystyrene foam ball
Brown chenille pipe cleaner for branch

To make the flower

1 Use the craft knife to cut the foam ball in half. Glue the polystyrene foam ball to a piece of cardboard or foam core for stability. Then use the small ball stylus to make a hole in the ball to hold the finished branch while drying. Set the ball aside.

2 Use the small scissors to cut a 3-inch (7.6 cm) length of the pipe cleaner.

3 Place the mini flowers on the art gum eraser and use the small ball stylus to cup each of them, following the instructions for cupping on page 15.

4 Use the tweezers to pick up one of the mini flowers by its outer edge, then dip the bottom of the flower into the glue. Try not to get too much glue on the flower, because it will flatten the shape. Place the flower at the top of the pipe cleaner and work downward. Repeat this step with all of the mini flowers, making sure you add flowers all around the pipe cleaner. You can

build on top of previously placed flowers to add fullness, but leave some of the pipe cleaner showing so that it looks like a branch. Leave about ½ inch (1.3 cm) of the pipe cleaner empty so that you can attach it to your bouquet.

5 Stick the pipe cleaner into the hole in the foam ball and let the piece dry for approximately 30 minutes. When it's dry, you can bend the piece so that it resembles a forsythia branch.

6 To make the leaves, refer to step 5 of the Aster project on page 31. Set the flower place in your arrangement, then add three to four leaves around the stem end to cover the pipe cleaner.

The gardenia has a dramatic fragrance and is frequently used in bridal bouquets. Botanist Carl Linnaeus named the flower in honor of the Scottish physician Dr. Alexander Garden.

GARDENIA

Level of difficulty: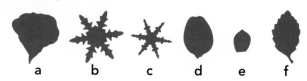

Punches for flower and quantity needed

6 super giant begonia petals for flower [a]
(For punch key and individual pieces used, see page 124.)

1 large snowflake for base of flower [b]

1 medium snowflake for base of flower [c]

6 large ovoid petals for flower [d]

2–3 small ovoid petals for flower [e]

Punch for leaves and quantity needed

3–4 large birch leaves [f]

a   b   c   d   e   f

Tools and Supplies

Basic Tool Kit (page 11)

Recommended cardstock colors:

  White or cream for begonia petals

  Medium green for large and medium
  snowflakes

  White or cream for large and small ovoid petals

  Dark green for birch leaves

Pigment ink pen in deep red

Gel pen in charcoal

GARDENIA

To make the flower

1 Punch the super giant begonia petals six times to produce a total of 30 petals. You'll only use the largest petals, so set the other shapes aside.

2 Place the begonia petals on the rubber mat and use the rounded end of the molding tool or the large ball stylus to shape them (refer to page 15 for shaping techniques). Then pinch and bend each of the petals, following the instructions for pinching and bending on page 16.

3 Place the large and medium snowflakes on the rubber mat and cup them, following the instructions for cupping on page 15. These shapes will be used to create the base of the flower.

4 Grasp one of the large begonia petals with the tweezers, then dip the small end of it into the glue and attach it to one of the projections on the large snowflake. Repeat with the rest of the begonia petals, attaching each to a projection on the large snowflake.

5 Use the tweezers to pick up the medium snowflake, apply glue to the bottom of it with the toothpick and set it in the center of the large snowflake.

6 Use the pigment ink pen to add a small amount of color to the base of the ovoid petals.

7 Place the large and small ovoid petals on the rubber mat and use the large ball stylus to shape them.

8 Pinch each of the large ovoid petals. Then grasp one of the large ovoid petals with the tweezers, dip the pinched end of it into the glue and place it on one of the projections on the medium snowflake. Place one large petal on each of the snowflake's projections.

9 Pinch the small end of two or three of the small ovoid petals. Then dip the pinched end of one of the petals into the glue and place it in the center of the flower, just outside the large ovoid petals. Repeat this step with the remaining small ovoid petals.

10 Let the flower dry for 10 to 15 minutes. Use your fingers or the tweezers to press the inner petals up.

11 Place one of the large birch leaves right-side up on the rubber mat, then use the gel pen to draw a stem line on the leaf. Turn the leaf over and use the small ball stylus to trace a stem line down its center. Shape as desired (refer to page 15 for shaping techniques). Repeat with the other leaves. Set the flower in place on your project, then tuck the leaves under it to finish.

GERBER DAISY

An attractive flower that draws bees, butterflies, and birds, this colorful blossom is widely used in bouquets. Choose your brightest and boldest papers to re-create the appeal of this vivid flower.

Level of difficulty: ✹ ✹

Punches for flower and quantity needed
3 super giant daisies for flower [a]
1 large daisy for flower [b]
2 medium suns for stamen [c]
3 small suns for stamen [d]

Punch for leaves and quantity needed
2–3 large oak leaves [e]

a   b   c   d   e

Tools and Supplies
Basic Tool Kit (page 11)
Recommended cardstock colors:
Red, yellow, orange, white, or magenta for super giant daisies
A shade that's lighter or darker than those listed above for large daisy
Bright yellow, green, or brownish red for stamen
Bright to medium green for leaves

To make the flower

1 Use the tweezers to pinch the petals of the three super giant daisies and the large daisy, following the instructions for pinching on page 16.

2 Place the super giant daisies on the rubber mat and use the rounded end of the molding tool to cup each one of them, following the instructions for cupping on page 15. Then use the large ball stylus to cup the large daisy.

3 Place one of the super giant daisies on the rubber mat to serve as a base. Use the tweezers to pick up another super giant daisy, then apply a small amount of glue to the bottom of it with the toothpick. Set this daisy on top of the base daisy, offsetting the petals. Repeat this technique for the third super giant daisy, then the large daisy. Use the tip of the tweezers to press down on the center of the daisies to secure all of the layers.

4 Use the small scissors to cut the rays of the two medium suns and two of the small suns in half. Use the tweezers to grasp each of the cut rays, then roll the rays toward the center of each of the suns, following the instructions for rolling on page 19.

5 Place the medium suns on the rubber mat and use the medium ball stylus to stir them, following the instructions for stirring on page 17. Pick up one of the suns with the tweezers, use the toothpick to apply a small amount of glue to the bottom of it and set it in the center of the flower. Repeat this step with the other medium sun.

6 Place the two small suns on the art gum eraser and cup them. Pick up one of the suns with the tweezers, then use the toothpick to apply a small amount of glue to the bottom of it. Set the sun in the center of the last medium sun. Repeat this step to add the second small sun.

7 Use the small scissors to cut ⅔ of the way into the third small sun, then grasp one side of the sun with the tweezers and roll it up as you did in step 4. Use the toothpick to apply a small amount of glue to the open side of the sun, then roll the shape up completely and hold it for a few seconds. Dip the bottom of the sun into the glue, then place it in the center of the last small sun.

8 To make the leaves, refer to step 5 of the Aster project on page 31.

HOLLY & BERRIES

This festive shrub is a favorite. The spine-tipped leaves and vibrant red berries are a welcome addition to paper wreaths, bouquets, and tags for the holiday season.

Level of difficulty:

Punches for leaves and quantity needed
3–4 large or mega giant holly leaves [a and b]

a   b

Tools and Supplies
Basic Tool Kit (page 11)
Recommended cardstock colors:
Dark to medium metallic green for holly leaves
Mulberry-colored paper for berries
Pigment ink pen in dark red

To make the flower

1 Place one of the large or mega giant holly leaves right-side down on the rubber mat. Use the small ball stylus to draw a stem line down the center of the leaf, then turn the leaf right-side up and retrace the stem line with the small stylus. (This is necessary when using metallic cardstock.) Repeat this step with the rest of the leaves.

2 Use the tweezers to grasp the stem end of one of the leaves and bend it upward along the stem line. Then dip the stem end into the glue and set the leaf in place in your project. Repeat this step with the remaining leaves.

To make the berries

3 Use the small scissors to cut a square that's approximately 1 x 1 inch (2.5 x 2.5 cm) for the mega giant holly leaf, or ½ x ½ inch (1.3 x 1.3 cm) for the large holly leaf from the mulberry paper.

4 Dip your index finger and thumb into the glue, making sure you don't pick up an excessive amount. Then use your sticky fingers to roll the square into a ball.

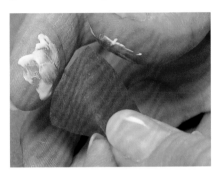

5 Repeat steps 3 and 4 to make the desired number of berries. Then use the pigment ink pen to add shading to the berries and set them in place with the holly leaves.

IMPATIENS

The impatiens has five petals and appears in shady gardens. Its name comes from the Latin word for impatient and refers to the explosive ejection of seed pods that occurs when the flower is touched. The impatiens is perfect as a fill-in for your paper bouquets.

Level of difficulty: ✺

Punches for flower and quantity needed
5 small impatiens leaves for petals [a]
1 small pinwheel for base of flower [b]

Punch for leaves and quantity needed
2–3 medium impatiens leaves [c]

a   b   c

Tools and Supplies
Basic Tool Kit (page 11)
Recommended cardstock colors:
   White, pink, orange, red, or light blue for small impatiens leaves
   Medium green for small pinwheel and medium impatiens leaves
   Small piece of cardstock in pale yellow, green, red, or white for center of flower

To make the flower

1 Use the small scissors to trim the stems from the five small impatiens leaves. Snip on either side of the stem to create the small divot the petal should have.

2 Place the small impatiens leaves on the rubber mat and use the rounded end of the molding tool or the large ball stylus to shape each of them into petals (refer to page 15 for shaping techniques). Then pinch and bend each of the petals, following the instructions for pinching and bending on page 16.

3 Place the pinwheel on the rubber mat and use the small ball stylus to cup it, following the instructions for cupping on page 15.

4 Use the small scissors to cut a strip of cardstock that's ⅛ x ½ inch (.3 x 1.3 cm). Hold one end of the strip with the tweezers, then use the toothpick to apply a small amount of glue to the opposite end of the strip. Roll the strip up around the tweezers. Hold the roll with your finger and thumb for a few seconds to secure it. Then

hold the shape with the tweezers and use the toothpick to apply a small amount of glue to the bottom of the roll. Set the roll in the center of the pinwheel.

5 Use the small ball stylus to gently hold the pinwheel in place on the rubber mat. Then pick up one of the impatiens petals with the tweezers and dip it into the glue. Place the petal on one of the projections of the pinwheel. Repeat this step with the remaining four small leaves.

6 To make the leaves for the flower from the medium impatiens leaves, refer to step 5 of the Aster project on page 31.

IRIS

One of many bulbs to appear in the spring, the iris has six petals that form in a typical fleur-de-lis pattern: three petals up and three petals down.

Level of difficulty: ✿ ✿

Punches for flower and quantity needed

3 mega lily petals for flower [a]
(For punch key and individual pieces used, see page 124.)

3 mega giant dahlia petals for flower [b]
(For punch key and individual pieces used, see page 124.)

1 medium snowflake for base of flower [c]

2 small sprig leaves for stamen [d]

Punch for leaves and quantity needed

4–6 mega elongated leaves [e]
(For punch key and individual pieces used, see page 124.)

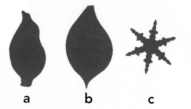

a   b   c   d   e

Tools and Supplies

Basic Tool Kit (page 11)

Recommended cardstock colors:

Deep to light purple, white, yellow, or orange for all petals

Bright yellow for stamen

Medium green for snowflake and leaves

Pigment ink markers in yellow, reddish brown, purple, and black

Gel ink pen in yellow (for use with dark cardstock only)

IRIS

To make the flower

1 Punch the mega lily petals three times to produce a total of 15 pieces. You will only use three of the petals. Then punch the mega giant dahlia petals three times for a total of 15 pieces. You will only use three of these petals.

2 Use the yellow pigment ink marker to shade the center of each petal, then use the reddish brown pigment ink marker to shade the yellow center.

If you are making a deep purple iris, use the yellow gel ink pen to shade the center of each petal, then use the purple or black pigment ink marker to shade the yellow center.

3 Place the three mega lily petals and the three mega giant dahlia petals on the rubber mat and use the concave end of the molding tool to shape each of them (refer to page 15 for shaping techniques). Then pinch the petals, following the instructions for pinching on page 16. Place the petals right-side down on the rubber mat and use the large ball stylus to shape the upper half of each of them.

4 Place the snowflake on the rubber mat and use the medium ball stylus to cup it, following the instructions for cupping on page 15.

5 Pinch and bend each of the six petals, following the instructions for pinching and bending on page 16.

6 Use the small ball stylus to hold the snowflake securely on the rubber mat. Then use the tweezers to grasp the top of one of the dahlia petals and dip the pinched end of it into the glue. Place the dahlia petal on one of the snowflake projections. Repeat with the other two dahlia petals, adding them to every other projection of the snowflake.

7 Pinch and bend the three lily petals once again. Then use the tweezers to grasp the top of one of the petals and dip the pinched end of the petal into the glue. Place the lily petal between two of the dahlia petals, holding the snowflake in place with the small ball stylus as you work. Repeat this step with the remaining lily petals. Let the shape dry for five to 10 minutes. Once the glue is set, you can easily bend the three lily petals up to form the fleur-de-lis shape.

8 Use the tweezers to grasp the bottom of one of the small sprig leaves, then use your thumb and index finger to pinch the leaf around the tweezers. Use the tweezers to hold onto the top of the sprig leaf and dip the bottom of it into the glue. Place the leaf in the center of the flower. Repeat this step with the second sprig leaf.

9 Punch the mega elongated leaves two times to produce six leaves. Add two or three mega elongated leaves to the iris by referring to step 5 of the Aster project on page 31.

PLACE SETTINGS

Place settings are the perfect accent for special occasion dinners, brunches, family reunions, and holiday get-togethers. You can easily make them using paper flowers as an embellishment. An 8½ x 11-inch (21.6 x 27.9 cm) piece of cardstock will produce six cards. Cut the paper lengthwise into three 3½-inch (8.9 cm) strips, then cut each strip into two 4-inch (10.2 cm) rectangles. Use a scoring board to divide and fold each rectangle in half. If desired, print the names of your guests onto the cards by hand, or use a computer to print them onto a patterned piece of paper that you can trim to fit the cards. Then add the paper flowers of your choice to the front of each card.

Complete your table setting by making napkin rings to match your place cards. Form a length of paper-coated wire into a circle that's large enough to hold your napkin. Then decorate the napkin ring with a favorite flower or a blossom that ties in with the season.

JAPANESE ANEMONE

The Japanese anemone blooms in the fall, adding an accent of pink, rose, or white to late gardens. The plant can grow to heights of five feet, and its leaves are lustrous and shiny. Pair the Japanese anemone with marigolds and asters to create a colorful paper bouquet for fall.

Level of difficulty: ❀ ❀

Punches for flower and quantity needed

1 medium snowflake for base of flower [a]
6 large ovoid petals for flower [b]
2 medium delicate snowflakes for stamen [c]
1 small sun for stamen [d]
1 small snowflake for stamen [e]

Punch for leaves and quantity needed

3–4 medium ivy leaves [f]

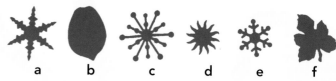

a   b   c   d   e   f

Tools and Supplies

Basic Tool Kit (page 11)
Recommended cardstock colors:
   Medium green for 1 medium snowflake
      and ivy leaves
   Various shades of pink or cream for petals
   Bright yellow for 2 medium delicate snowflakes
      and small snowflake
   Black for small sun
Chalk in a shade deeper than petal cardstock
   (optional)

To make the flower

1 Place the medium green snow-flake on the rubber mat and use the large ball stylus to cup it, following the instructions for cupping on page 15. Set the pieces aside.

2 Optional: Use the chalk in a deeper hue to shade the petals.

3 Place the six large ovoid petals on the rubber mat and use the round end of the molding tool or the large ball stylus to shape them (refer to page 15 for shaping techniques). Then pinch and bend each of the petals, following the instructions for pinching and bending on page 16.

4 Place the medium green snowflake on the rubber mat as a base and use the small ball stylus to hold it in place. Then use the tweezers to pick up one of the petals, dip the pinched end of it into the glue and place the petal on one of the snowflake's projections. Add one petal to each projection on the snowflake.

5 Place one of the bright yellow medium delicate snowflakes on the art gum eraser and use the small ball stylus to cup it. Grasp it with the tweezers, use the toothpick to apply a small amount of glue to the bottom of it and set it in the center of the flower. Repeat this step with the second medium delicate snow-flake, pressing down in the center of the piece with the tip of the tweezers to secure the layers.

6 Use the small scissors to cut the rays of the small black sun in half. Place the sun on the art gum eraser and use the small ball stylus to cup it. Grasp the sun with the tweezers, use the toothpick to apply a small amount of glue to the bottom of it, then place it in the center of the flower, on top of the snowflake from step 5.

7 Place the small snowflake on the art gum eraser and use the small ball stylus to cup it. Grasp the shape with the tweezers, use the toothpick to apply a small amount of glue to the bottom of it and place it in the center of the small sun. Use the tip of the tweezers to press down on the center of the piece to secure all the layers.

8 To add the leaves, refer to step 8 of the Anemone project on page 28.

MARIGOLD

These pompom-like flowers belong to the daisy family. They are noticeably aromatic, and their pinnate leaves make them distinctive in the garden. Although they take a little extra time to create in paper, their unique beauty makes the effort worthwhile.

Level of difficulty: 🌸 🌸 🌸

Punches for flower and quantity needed

4 small hearts for petals [a]
2 medium cosmos for flower [b]
4 silhouette daisies for flower [c]
2 small daisies for flower [d]
16 small pears for petals [e]
16 small teardrops for petals [f]
1 mayflower for petals [g]

Punch for leaves and quantity needed

3–4 large oak or dusty miller leaves [h]

a   b   c   d

e   f   g   h

Tools and Supplies

Basic Tool Kit (page 11)

Recommended cardstock colors:

Yellow, orange, red, or rust for cosmos, daisies, pears, teardrops, hearts, and mayflower

Bright or olive green for leaves

Pigment ink pen in red, brownish red, or yellowish gold

To make the flower

1 With the small scissors, cut the four small hearts in half to make eight petals.

2 Use the pigment ink pen in a contrasting color to shade the 16 small pears, the 16 small teardrops, the eight petals, one of the silhouette daisies, the two small daisies, and the mayflower. Set the pieces aside.

3 Place the two medium cosmos and the four silhouette daisies on the rubber mat and use the large ball stylus or the round end of the molding tool to cup the shapes, following the instructions for cupping on page 15. Then place the two small daisies and mayflower on the art gum eraser and use the small ball stylus to cup them. Set the pieces aside.

4 Place the 16 small pears on the rubber mat and use the large ball stylus to shape them (refer to page 15 for shaping techniques). Pinch and bend each of the pears, following the instructions for pinching and bending on page 16. Then grasp one of the pears with the tweezers, dip the stem end of it into the glue and attach it to a petal on one of the cosmos. Repeat this step with all 16 of the pears to fill the two cosmos.

5 Place the 16 teardrops on the rubber mat and use the large ball stylus to shape them. Then pinch and bend each of the teardrops. Grasp one of the teardrops with the tweezers, dip the small end of it into the glue and attach it to a petal on one of the cupped silhouette daisies. Repeat this step with all 16 of the teardrops to fill two of the silhouette daisies.

6 Place the eight petals cut from the four hearts on the rubber mat and use the large ball stylus to shape them. Then pinch and bend each of the petals. Grasp one of the petals with the tweezers, dip the small end of it into the glue and attach it to a petal on the third cupped silhouette daisy. Repeat this step with all of the petals to fill the third silhouette daisy.

To build the flower

7 Place one of the cosmos/pear layers on the rubber mat to serve as a base. Pick up the second cosmos/pear layer with the tweezers and use a toothpick to apply glue to the bottom of it. Set this layer on top of the base, offsetting the petals.

8 Use the tweezers to pick up one of the silhouette daisy/teardrop petal layers, then use the toothpick to apply glue to the bottom of the layer. Set this layer on top of the last cosmos/pear layer, offsetting the petals. Repeat this step with the remaining two silhouette daisy/teardrop petal combinations.

9 Use the tweezers to pick up the silhouette daisy/heart petal layer, then use a toothpick to apply glue to the bottom of the layer. Set it on top of the last silhouette/teardrop petal layer, offsetting the petals.

10 To add the next layer, use the tweezers to pick up the silhouette daisy that you shaded with the pigment ink pen in step 2. Then use the toothpick to apply glue to the bottom of it and set it on top of the last silhouette daisy/heart petal layer, offsetting the petals.

11 For the next layer, use the tweezers to pick up one of the small daisies. Then use the toothpick to apply glue to the bottom of it and place it on top of the single silhouette flower.

12 To create the next layer, pick up the mayflower with the tweezers and use the toothpick to apply glue to the bottom of it. Then place it on top of the small daisy.

13 For the final layer, pick up the small daisy with the tweezers, use the toothpick to apply glue to the bottom of it, and set it on top of the mayflower. Use the tip of the tweezers to press down on the center of the flower to secure all of the layers.

14 To make the large oak or medium dusty miller leaves, refer to step 5 of the Aster project on page 31.

STRAW HAT

What gardening enthusiast wouldn't love to have a straw hat adorned with his or her favorite flowers? Choose a grosgrain ribbon that is 1 to 1½ inches (2.5 to 3.8 cm) wide, depending on the height of the brim. (Adding ribbon to hold the paper blossoms will allow you to change the band of flowers with each season.) Measure the circumference of the brim, cut the ribbon so that it's 2 to 3 inches (5 to 7.6 cm) longer, then wrap the ribbon around the brim and secure it with a brad, hook-and-loop tape, or a snap. Decorate the hat with your favorite paper flowers to create a wearable work of art, or display the finished product on a wall.

ORNAMENTAL KALE

This little jewel is usually plant-ed alongside chrysanthemums or asters to add a bold statement to a sleeping garden in fall and winter. Include it in your fall paper bouquets for a bit of extra interest.

Level of difficulty: ✿ ✿

Punches for flower and quantity needed

30 mega giant snapdragon petals for flower [a]
(For punch key and individual pieces used, see page 124.)

1 large snowflake for base of flower [b]

1 medium snowflake for base of flower [c]

a   b   c

Tools and Supplies

Basic Tool Kit (page 11)

Recommended cardstock colors:

Cream, light or dark green, or various shades of purple for snapdragon petals and snowflakes

Chalk for shading in coordinating colors

To make the flower

1 Punch the snapdragon petals six times to produce a total of 30 petals. You won't use all of the shapes. If you are creating a variegated variety of kale, punch the snapdragon petals in contrasting colors of cardstock. You can use the chalk to shade the center of some of the largest petals, then mix the petals into the finished flower.

2 Place the large and medium snowflakes on the rubber mat and use the large ball stylus to cup them, following the instructions for cupping on page 15. Set the pieces aside.

3 Place the largest snapdragon petals on the rubber mat and use the rounded end of the molding tool or the large ball stylus to shape them (refer to page 15 for shaping techniques). Then pinch and bend each of the petals, following the instructions for pinching and bending on page 16. Set the petals aside.

4 Place the large snowflake on the rubber mat. Then pick up one of the largest snapdragon petals with the tweezers, dip the end of it into the glue and attach it to one of the projections on the large snowflake. Repeat this step with all of the largest petals.

5 Use the tweezers to pick up the medium snowflake, then, apply a small amount of glue to the bottom of it with the toothpick. Place it in the center of the large snowflake, then press down on the snowflakes with the tip of the tweezers to secure them.

6 Repeat step 4 to add the next largest petals to the projections on the medium snowflake.

7 Add two or three more rows of graduated-sized petals as you did in step 4. End with the smallest petals in the center.

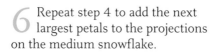

PANSY

The pansy has five petals with very distinctive shading on the three top petals. The name of the flower is derived from the French word pensée, which means thought. The name was inspired by the fact that the blossom looks something like a human face, and during the month of August, it droops forward as though lost in thought.

Level of difficulty: ✿ ✿

Punches for flower and quantity needed

5 super giant begonia petals for flower [a]
(For punch key and individual pieces used, see page 124.)

1 mini star for stamen [b]

1 medium snowflake for base of flower [c]

Punch for leaves and quantity needed

3–4 medium birch leaves [d]

a   b   c   d

Tools and Supplies

Basic Tool Kit (page 11)

Recommended cardstock colors:

Lavender, deep purple, yellow, white, or various shades of pink for petals

Yellow for mini star

Medium green for snowflake and leaves

Pigment ink marker in purple, brownish red, or black, depending on your choice of cardstock

Gel pen in yellow (for shading dark cardstock)

To make the flower

1 Punch the super giant begonia petals three times. You should have a total of 15 petals, although you won't need all of them to make the flower.

2 Use the pigment marker or gel pen to add shade lines to one of the medium begonia petals and two of the small begonia petals.

3 Place the snowflake on the rubber mat and use the medium ball stylus to cup it, following the instructions for cupping on page 15.

4 Place the two small begonia petals from step 2 and all three medium begonia petals on the rubber mat and use the large ball stylus or the concave end of the molding tool to shape them (refer to page 15 for shaping techniques).

5 Pinch and bend each of the petals, following the instructions for pinching and bending on page 16.

6 Use the small ball stylus to hold the snowflake securely on the rubber mat. Then use the tweezers to pick up one of the unshaded medium petals, dip the pinched end of it into the glue and place it at the top left side of the snowflake. Repeat this step with the second medium unshaded petal, placing it at the top right side of the snowflake, overlapping the first medium petal slightly.

7 Use the tweezers to pick up one of the small shaded petals, dip the pinched end of it into the glue and place it on the left side of the snowflake, just below the large petal. Repeat this step with the second small shaded petal, placing it on the right side, just below the medium petal.

8 Use the tweezers to pick up the medium shaded petal, dip the pinched end of it into the glue and place it in the center of the flower with the outer end facing down from the other four petals.

9 Place the mini star on the art gum eraser and use the small ball stylus to cup it. Use the tweezers to pick up the star at the top, then add a small amount of glue to the bottom of it with the toothpick. Place the star in the center of the flower.

10 Place one of the large birch leaves right-side down on the rubber mat, then use the small ball stylus to create a stem line down the center of the leaf. Turn the leaf over and add vein lines from the stem line out to the edge. Shape as desired (refer to page 15 for shaping techniques). Repeat this step with the other leaves. Set the flowers in place on your project, then tuck the leaves under it to finish.

Peony

This large, showy flower starts blooming in the spring in most locations, but it continues to flourish well into the early summer, providing a wonderful burst of color in the garden.

Level of difficulty: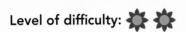

Punches for flower and quantity needed
12 medium apples for flower [a]
2 large snowflakes for base of flower [b]
3 medium suns for stamen [c]
3 small suns for stamen [d]

Punch for leaves and quantity needed
3–4 medium grape leaves [e]

a   b   c   d   e

Tools and Supplies
Basic Tool Kit (page 11)
Recommended cardstock colors:
  Red, white, or various shades of pink for apples
  Green for large snowflake
  Yellow for medium and small suns
  Medium to dark green for leaves
Pigment ink marker and/or chalk in yellow,
  or a shade that's deeper than cardstock used
  for apples

To make the flower

1 Cut the stems from each of the apple shapes, then use the chalk or pigment ink marker to shade the smaller end of each apple.

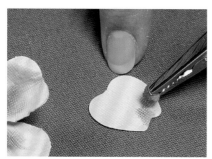

2 Place the apple shapes right-side up on the rubber mat with the large ends of the shapes pointing away from you. Then use the large ball stylus or rounded end of the molding tool to shape each of the apples (refer to page 113 for the shaping technique used in the Tulip project).

3 Place the two snowflakes on the rubber mat and use the large ball stylus to cup them, following the instructions for cupping on page 15.

4 Pinch and bend each of the apples, following the instructions for pinching and bending on page 16.

5 Use the small ball stylus to hold one of the snowflakes securely on the rubber mat. Then use the tweezers to pick up one of the apples, dip the stem end of it into the glue and place it on one of the snowflake projections. Repeat this step with all of the apples until both snowflakes are covered. Let the two snowflakes dry for two to five minutes.

6 Dip the bottom of one of the snowflakes into the glue and attach it to the other snowflake, off-setting the petals between the two layers. Use the tip of the tweezers to press down on the center of the snowflakes while they're on the rubber mat. This step will re-cup the shape of the flower.

7 Use the small scissors to cut each ray of the three medium suns in half, making sure you cut a little farther into the center on every other ray. Then use the tweezers to roll the cut rays toward the center of each sun. Place the suns on the rubber mat and use the medium ball stylus to stir them, following the instructions for stirring on page 17.

8 Repeat step 7 with two of the small suns.

9 Use the small scissors to cut two-thirds of the way into the center of the remaining small sun. Then use the tweezers to grasp one of the ends of the sun and roll the shape counterclockwise into a cone, following the instructions for rolling on page 19. Apply a small dab of glue to the unrolled end, then close up the cone. Hold the shape with the tweezers until the glue sets, for approximately one minute.

10 Use the toothpick to apply a dab of glue to the bottom of one of the medium suns, then attach it to the flower. Press down on the center of the sun with the tweezers to secure it. Then layer the remaining two medium suns, one on top of the other, in the center of the flower in the same manner.

11 Repeat step 10 with the two small suns from step 8. The cone-shaped sun from step 9 should be the last one you set in the center of the flower.

12 Place one of the grape leaves right-side down on the rubber mat. Use the small ball stylus to add a stem line down the center of the leaf, then turn the piece over and add vein lines from the stem line to the outside edge. Shape as desired (refer to page 15 for shaping techniques). Repeat this step with the remaining leaves. Set the flower in place on your project, then tuck the leaves under it to finish.

PERIWINKLE

This five-petal flower commonly serves as a ground cover. Some species are used in drugs for treating Hodgkin's Disease and lymphocytic leukemia. The flower is simple to make in paper and—just like its real counterpart—a great fill-in flower for any bouquet.

Level of difficulty:

Punches for flower and quantity needed
1 super giant violet/iris for flower [a]
(For punch key and individual pieces used, see page 124.)

Punch for leaves and quantity needed
2–3 medium birch leaves [b]
1–2 medium twigs [c]

a   b   c

Tools and Supplies
Basic Tool Kit (page 11)
Recommended cardstock colors:
White, lilac, blue, red, or various shades of pink for violet/iris
Dark green for leaves and twigs
Gel pen in white
Glitter glue in yellow

To make the flower

1 Punch the super giant violet/iris one time. Then place the violet shape on the rubber mat and use the white gel pen to shade the center of it. Let the piece dry.

3 To create the small center of the flower, use a small drop of yellow glitter glue. Let the glue set before adding the periwinkle to your project.

2 Place the violet right-side down on the rubber mat and use the rounded end of the molding tool or the large ball stylus to shape it (refer to page 15 for shaping techniques). Turn the violet right-side up and use the small ball stylus to cup it, following the instructions for cupping on page 15.

4 To add the leaves and twigs, refer to step 5 of the Aster project on page 31.

PETUNIA

A summer garden or patio wouldn't be the same without this easy-growing annual. The flower's name comes from the French word petun, *meaning tobacco, to which the petunia is botanically related. The flower can be easily coordinated with other summer paper blossoms.*

Level of difficulty:

Punches for flower and quantity needed

1 medium sun for base of flower [a]

5 super giant begonia petals for flower [b]

(For punch key and individual pieces used, see page 124.)

Punch for leaves and quantity needed

3–4 birch leaves [c]

a   b   c

Tools and Supplies

Basic Tool Kit (page 11)

Recommended cardstock colors:

Medium green for medium sun and leaves

White, light blue, and various shades of pink or purple for petals

Pigment ink pen in a shade that's deeper than petals

Small scrap of cardstock in a shade that's deeper than petals

To make the flower

1 Use the small scissors to cut approximately two-thirds of the way into the center of the medium sun. Grasp one side of the sun with the tweezers and roll it into a cone. Use the toothpick to apply a dab of glue to the other end of the sun before closing the shape completely. Use the tweezers to hold the shape until it's set.

2 Use the pigment ink pen to shade the small end of all petals.

3 Place the five begonia petals on the rubber mat and use the round end of the molding tool or the large ball stylus to shape them (refer to page 15 for shaping techniques).

4 Pinch and bend each of the petals, following the instructions for pinching and bending on page 16.

5 Use your thumb and index finger to pick up one of the petals, then dip the end of it into the glue. Place the petal on the cone-shaped sun. Repeat this step to add all of the petals, overlapping them slightly on the cone shape.

6 Cut the scrap of cardstock into a strip that's 1/16 x 1 inch (1.6 x 25 mm). Grasp one end of the strip with the tweezers, then roll it up around the tweezers. Use the toothpick to apply a small amount of glue to the end of the roll to secure it. Place the roll in the center of the flower.

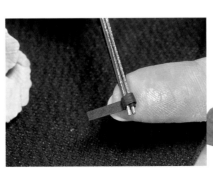

7 Place one of the medium birch leaves right-side down on the rubber mat. Use the small ball stylus to make a stem line down the center of the leaf. Turn the leaf over and add vein lines. Shape as desired (refer to page 15 for shaping techniques). Repeat this step with all of the leaves. Set the flower in place on your project, then tuck the leaves under it to finish.

PINECONES & BOUGHS

Swags and wreaths of pine boughs with pinecones are symbols of the holiday season that comfort us with their refreshing aroma. Add them to your paper bouquet for a natural look.

Level of difficulty: ✹ ✹

Punches for pinecone and quantity needed
18–20 small pears for pinecone scales [a]
3–4 mega ferns [b]
2–4 pine boughs [c]

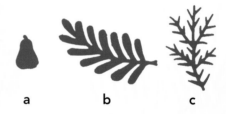

a   b   c

Tools and Supplies
Basic Tool Kit (page 11)
Recommended cardstock colors:
    Medium to dark brown or taupe for pears
    Dark green for mega ferns
    Silvery dark green for pine boughs
Small wooden stick
Molding paste glue
   (Tip: The paste glue dries clear but very slowly. It's best to make your pinecones a day ahead to allow the glue to completely dry.)
3-inch (7.6 cm) square of polyester film
Clay spatula

To make the pinecone

1 Use the wooden stick to scoop out a blob of molding paste that's approximately ⅜ to ½ inch (1 to 1.3 cm). Place the paste on the square of polyester film, then use your fingers to smooth the paste into a beehive shape.

2 Place the small pears right-side down on the rubber mat and use the large ball stylus to shape them (refer to page 15 for shaping techniques). Turn the pears over, then pinch and bend each of them, following the instructions for pinching and bending on page 16.

3 Grasp the large end of one of the pears with the tweezers and place it on the glue beehive in an upright position. Add a row of seven pears around the glue base.

4 Repeat step 3, placing the next row of pears above the previous row on the glue base. You should create four rows of pears on the glue cone.

5 Use the tweezers to roll one last pear shape diagonally. Then grasp the roll with the tweezers and place it in the top center of the cone.

6 Use the clay spatula to transfer the completed cone to your project. (Tip: Don't let the cone dry on the polyester film.)

To make the pine boughs

7 Use the small scissors to cut the fronds on one of the ferns in half. Grasp the fern with the tweezers and bend it upward, then use the fingers of your free hand to fluff out the fronds. Dip the end of the fern into the glue and place it in the cluster of pinecones. Repeat this step with all of the ferns.

8 Grasp the pine bough with the tweezers and bend the needles up with your free hand. Dip the end of the bough into the glue and add it to the ferns.

POINSETTIA

Native to Mexico, the poinsettia was introduced to the United States by Joel Poinsett in 1895. The construction of this flower is unique compared to the other blossoms in the book. The leaves of the poinsettia look like petals, while the flower is a center seed cluster that is re-created in glitter glue.

Level of difficulty: ✿ ✿

Punches for poinsettia and quantity needed

3 medium snowflakes for base of poinsettia [a]

6 mega giant dahlia petals for bottom layer of leaves [b]

(For punch key and individual pieces used, see page 124.)

15 mega giant dahlia petals for top layer of leaves [c]

1 small sun for stamen [d]

2 small stamens [e]

a   b   c   d   e

Tools and Supplies

Basic Tool Kit (page 11)

Recommended cardstock colors:

    Medium green for medium snowflakes

    Various shades of green for bottom layer of leaves

    Red, yellow, white, or various shades of pink for top layer of leaves

    Yellow for small sun

    Bright green for small stamens

Chalks for shading

Pearlescent watercolor paint

Water reservoir brush

Glitter glue in red and yellow

To make the flower

1 Place the medium snowflakes on the rubber mat and use the large ball stylus to cup them, following the instructions for cupping on page 15. Set the snowflakes aside.

2 Punch the mega giant dahlia petals two times from the green cardstock to produce the bottom layer of leaves. You should have a total of 10 petals, but you'll only use the six largest petals to form the bottom layer of leaves.

3 Place the six largest green dahlia petals right-side down on the rubber mat and use the round end of the molding tool to shape them into leaves (refer to page 15 for shaping techniques). Then use the small ball stylus to add a stem line down the center of each leaf. Turn the leaves over and use the small ball stylus to add vein lines from the stem line to the outer edge of each leaf.

4 Pinch and bend each of the six leaves, following the instructions for pinching and bending on page 16.

5 Place one of the cupped snowflakes on the rubber mat and use the small ball stylus to hold it securely. Then use the tweezers to pick up one of the large green leaves, dip the pinched end of it into the glue and attach it to the snowflake projection. Repeat this step with the other five large green leaves.

6 Punch the mega giant dahlia petals three times from your choice of colored cardstock to produce a total of 15 petals. Choose 12 of the petals in varying sizes to form the next two layers of the flower. Repeat steps 3 through 5 with these petals, attaching six petals to each of the two remaining cupped snowflakes. Let the pieces dry for five minutes.

7 Place the snowflake with the base layer of green leaves on the rubber mat. Then use the toothpick to apply glue to the bottom of one of the snowflakes from step 6 and place it on top of the base snowflake, offsetting the petals. Press down slightly in the center of the snowflakes with the tip of the tweezers. Repeat this process with the last snowflake, offsetting the petals and pressing down on the center of the piece with the tip of the tweezers.

8 Use the small scissors to cut the rays of the small sun in half. Place the sun on the rubber mat and use the medium ball stylus to stir it, following the instructions for stirring on page 17. Then use the toothpick to apply a small amount of glue to the bottom of the sun and set it in the center of the layered snowflakes.

9 Place the small stamens on the art gum eraser and use the small ball stylus to cup them. Use your forefinger and thumb to squeeze each of the shapes together to tighten the cupping. Then use a toothpick to apply a small amount of glue to the bottoms of each of the stamens. With the tweezers, place the stamens side-by-side in the center of the sun shape.

10 Apply small amounts of the glitter glue to the tips of the stamens to complete the flower.

PRIMROSE

This well-known perennial is a native to the northern hemisphere. Depending on the variety, the primrose may have five or more petals that are notched at the tips. The flower comes in many different colors, which makes it a great border plant for the garden.

Level of difficulty: ✿ ✿

Punches for flower and quantity needed
1 large blossom for flower [a]
5 small sakuras for use with dark-colored flowers [b]
1 small pinwheel for base of flower [c]
1 mini snowflake for stamen [d]
1 mini sun for stamen [e]

Punch for leaves and quantity needed
3 super giant moth orchids [f]
(For punch key and individual pieces used, see page 124.)

a   b   c   d   e   f

Tools and Supplies
Basic Tool Kit (page 11)
Recommended cardstock colors:
   Yellow, red, orange, deep purple, or peach for blossom
   Medium green for pinwheel
   Bright green for snowflake
   Yellow for mini sun
   Medium to dark green for leaves
Sheet of text weight paper in bright yellow for sakuras
Pencil
Pigment marker pens in red, indigo blue, and bright yellow
Acid-free glue stick

To make the flower

1 If you are using lighter colored cardstock (yellow, orange, or peach) for the blossom, use the contrasting pigment marker to shade the center of the blossom.

If you are using darker colored cardstock (red, deep purple, or scarlet) for the blossom, shade the five small sakuras with the contrast-ing pigment ink marker Use the glue stick to adhere one of the sakuras to one of the petals on the blossom. Repeat this step with the rest of the sakuras. Let the blossom dry for five to 10 minutes.

If you choose to color the petals to achieve dark colors with bright center shading, use the pigment ink marker as follows:

(a) Punch the large blossom in yellow, then sketch or trace a star shape in the middle of the piece with a pencil. Color the star shape in with the bright yellow pigment ink marker. Then color around the star shape with the red pigment ink marker until the outer portion of each petal is completely colored in.

(b) Punch the large blossom in white or cream, then sketch or trace a star shape in the middle of the piece with a pencil. Color the star shape in with the bright yellow pigment ink marker, then color around the star shape with the indigo blue pigment ink marker until the outer portion of each petal is completely colored in.

2 Use the small scissors to cut the large blossom into five separate petals.

3 Place the five petals on the rubber mat and use the large ball stylus or the concave, half-moon end of the molding tool to shape them (refer to page 15 for shaping techniques). Then pinch and bend each of the petals, following the instructions for pinching and bending on page 16.

4 Place the small pinwheel on the rubber mat and use the small ball stylus to cup it, following the instructions for cupping on page 15.

5 Use the small ball stylus to hold the pinwheel securely on the rubber mat. Then use the tweezers to pick up a petal, dip the end of it into the glue and attach it to one of the projections on the pinwheel. Repeat this step with the remaining four petals.

6 Place the mini snowflake on the art gum eraser and use the small ball stylus to cup it. Use the tweezers to grasp the snowflake at the top, then use the toothpick to apply a small amount of the glue to the bottom of it. Attach the mini snowflake to the center of the flower.

7 Use the small scissors to cut ⅔ of the way through the center of the mini sun. Then use the tweezers to grasp one side of the cut sun and roll it counterclockwise, leaving a small area unrolled. Use the toothpick to apply glue to the unrolled area, then close the shape. Hold the piece for one to two minutes to set the glue, then attach the sun to the center of the mini snowflake.

8 Punch the super giant moth orchid three times to produce 15 pieces. You will only use three of the pieces for the leaves. To add the leaves, refer to step 5 of the Aster project on page 31.

Queen Anne's Lace

Queen Anne's Lace is also known as wild carrot, because the carrots we eat today were once cultivated from this plant. The delicate, lacy flower will add a sweet touch to your paper bouquets.

Level of difficulty:

Punches for flower and quantity needed
6 large sparkles for base of flower [a]
60–65 mini snowflakes for flower [b]

Punch for leaves and quantity needed
3–4 large oak leaves [c]

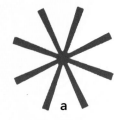 a b c

Tools and Supplies
Basic Tool Kit (page 11)
Recommended cardstock colors:
Bright to medium green for sparkles and leaves
Creamy white for snowflakes
Gel pen in yellow

To make the flower

1 Use the small scissors to cut the projections on three of the large sparkles in half.

2 Place the three sparkles on the rubber mat and use the medium ball stylus to cup them, following the instructions for cupping on page 15. Set the sparkles aside.

3 Place one of the uncut sparkles on the rubber mat as a base. Use the tweezers to pick up one of the cut sparkles, dip it into the glue, then set it on top of the base sparkle. Repeat this step, alternating between cut and uncut sparkles, until all of the sparkles have been set in place. Use the tip of the tweezers to press down on the center of the layers to set them. Let the piece dry for five to 10 minutes.

4 Place all of the mini snow-flakes on the rubber mat and use the point of the yellow gel pen to cup them.

5 Pick up one of the cupped snowflakes with the tweezers, use the toothpick to apply a small amount of glue to the bottom of it, then place it on one of the sparkle projections. Repeat this step until you have covered most of the sparkle base with snowflakes.

6 To add the large oak leaves, refer to step 5 of the Aster project on page 31.

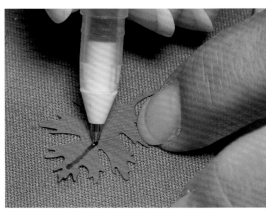

RHODODENDRON

This genus boasts over 800 species and is always a favorite in landscaping projects. The eye-catching flowers are late spring bloomers. They come in a range of spectacular colors—pick your favorite shade and replicate it in paper.

Level of difficulty:

Punches for flower and quantity needed
18 medium sakuras for flower [a]
18 small cosmos for stamens [b]

Punch for leaves and quantity needed
3–4 super giant cymbidium orchids [c]
(For punch key and individual pieces used, see page 124.)

a   b   c

Tools and Supplies
Basic Tool Kit (page 11)
Recommended cardstock colors:
 Lavender, yellow, orange, or various shades of pink and red for sakuras
 A lighter shade for cosmos
 Dark green for leaves
Craft knife
Polystyrene foam ball, 1½-inch (3.8 cm) diameter
Dark green mulberry paper
Decoupage paste
Pigment marker pen in a shade that contrasts with cosmos

To make the flower

1 Use the craft knife to cut the foam ball in half. Use the small scissors to cut a circle from the mulberry paper that's approximately 3 inches (7.6 cm) in diameter, then adhere the circle to the top of the foam ball with the glue or the decoupage paste. Let the piece dry for five to 10 minutes before proceeding with the next steps.

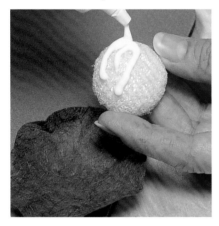

2 Use the small scissors to make ¼-inch (6 mm) cuts in between the petals of the sakuras.

3 Place the sakura right-side down on the rubber mat and use the rounded end of the molding tool or the large ball stylus to shape it (refer to page 15 for shaping techniques). Turn the shape right-side up, place it on the art gum eraser and use the medium ball stylus to cup it, following the instructions for cupping on page 15.

4 Use the pigment ink marker to tip the ends of one of the cosmos on both sides. Then use the small scissors to cut each petal of the cosmos in half, place it on the art gum eraser and cup it, following the instructions for cupping on page 15.

5 Use the toothpick to add a small amount of glue to the center of the cosmos and pinch it closed at the base for about one minute to allow the glue to set. Use your fingers to fluff out the closed cosmos.

6 Use the tweezers to pick up the sakura, dip the bottom of it into the glue and set it on the foam ball at the outer edge.

7 Use the tweezers to pick up the closed cosmos, then place it in the center of the sakura.

Repeat steps 2 to 7 to make approximately 17 more flowers to cover the foam ball completely.

8 Punch the super giant cymbidium orchid four times to produce 20 pieces. You will only use three or four of the pieces for the leaves. Add three to four leaves to the rhododendron by referring to step 5 of the Aster project on page 31.

ROSE

The floribunda species of rose blooms from summer to early fall. It is one of the many modern garden roses that proliferated in the early twentieth century. Experiment with chalks or pigment ink pens to add interest to the petals of your paper rose.

Level of difficulty: ✿ ✿

Punches for flower and quantity needed

14–15 super giant begonia petals for flower [a]
(For punch key and individual pieces used, see page 124.)
1 large snowflake for base of flower [b]
3 medium snowflakes for stamen [c]
1 small sun for stamen [d]

Punch for leaves and quantity needed

6 mega giant garden leaves [e]
(For punch key and individual pieces used, see page 124.)

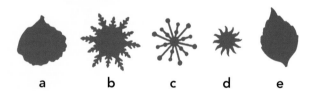

a   b   c   d   e

Tools and Supplies

Basic Tool Kit (page 11)
Recommended cardstock colors:
   Red, yellow, or various shades of pink for petals
   Medium to dark green for large snowflake
   Bright yellow for medium snowflakes and small sun
   Medium to dark green for leaves
Chalk in color to complement cardstock
Pigment ink pen in reddish brown

Rose

To make the flower

1 Punch the super giant begonia petals six times in your chosen cardstock color to produce a total of 30 petals. You won't need the two smallest petals, so set those shapes aside.

2 Place the large snowflake on the rubber mat and use the round end of the molding tool to shape it (refer to page 15 for shaping techniques). A slight cupping effect will develop as you shape the snowflake.

3 Place the begonia petals wrong-side up on the rubber mat and use the round end of the molding tool or the large ball stylus to shape them. Turn the petals right-side up and shape them again. Then pinch and bend each of the petals, following the instructions for pinching and bending on page 16.

4 If you are creating a variegated variety of rose, use the chalk to shade the outer edge of the petals.

5 Pick out the largest begonia petals. Dip the small end of one of the petals into the glue and place it on a projection of the large snowflake. Repeat this step until you have added six petals to the snowflake.

6 Pick out the second largest begonia petals. Pick up one of the petals with the tweezers, dip the pinched end of it into the glue and place it inside the first row of petals, offsetting it. Use a total of five petals to create this row.

7 Pick out the third largest begonia petals. Repeat step 6 to add the petals to the inside of the second row, offsetting the petals as you work. Use a total of three to four petals to create this row.

8 Use the reddish brown pigment ink pen to dot the ends of the medium snowflakes. Then use the pen to tip the ends of the small sun.

9 Use the small scissors to cut the rays of the small sun in half.

10 Place the medium snow-flakes and the sun on the art gum eraser and use the small ball stylus to cup them, following the instructions for cupping on page 15. Use the tweezers to pick up one of the medium snowflakes, then, use the toothpick to apply a small amount of glue to the bottom of it. Set it in the center of the flower. Repeat this step with the remaining two medium snowflakes. Then add the small sun.

11 Punch the mega giant garden leaves two times to produce a total of six leaves. Place the leaves right-side down on the rubber mat. Use the small ball stylus to draw a stem line down the center of each leaf. Then turn the leaves right-side up and use the small ball stylus to add vein lines to each of them, from the stem line to the edge. Shape each leaf as desired (refer to page 15 for shaping techniques). Set the flower in place on your project, then tuck the leaves under it to finish.

SWEET PEA

This fragrant, delicate climbing flower doesn't last long in the garden. Make the sweet pea from paper, and you can enjoy it throughout the year. Try punching the shapes from coffee filters to recreate the delicate feel of this flower.

Level of difficulty:

Punches for flower and quantity needed
  1 mega sweet pea for flower [a]
  1 small snowflake for base of flower [b]

Punch for leaves and quantity needed
  3–4 medium chestnut leaves [c]

a   b   c

Tools and Supplies
  Basic Tool Kit (page 11)
  Recommended cardstock colors:
    Bright green for small snowflake
    Bright to medium green for leaves
  Coffee filter
  Aluminum foil
  Paper towel
  Pearlescent watercolor paint
  Water reservoir brush
  Chalk
  Scrap of cardstock in bright green for tendrils

To make the flower

1 Punch the sweet pea shape from the coffee filter, then place the piece on the aluminum foil. Paint the piece with watercolor paint, then transfer it to a paper towel and let it dry. If you prefer, use the chalk to color the shape instead of the paint. (You can also make sweet peas from cardstock, if you desire. Choose blue, red, white, purple, or pink cardstock.)

2 Place the sweet pea shape right-side up on the rubber mat with the larger end at the top. Set the large ball stylus on the outer edge of the piece, then draw the stylus toward the center of the piece to shape it. Use enough pressure to wrinkle the coffee filter paper, but don't tear it.

3 Leave the sweet pea on the rubber mat and use the large ball stylus to stroke down on the center bud. Then use the stylus to shape the wing-like petals (refer to page 15 for shaping techniques).

4 Use the thumb and index fingers of both hands to grasp the wing-like petals of the sweet pea. Then fold the bottom half of the sweet pea up towards the large fan-like petal and press it inward. To secure the two sections, use the toothpick to apply a bit of glue to the joint between the upper and lower sections. You may need to use the small ball stylus or the toothpick to hold the piece until it sets.

5 Use the toothpick to apply a bit of glue to the lower portions of both of the wing-like petals, then use the tweezers to clamp the two petals together, so that the lower, glued portions meet. Let the piece dry for 15 to 20 minutes, then continue bending the petals to make them look natural if you desire.

6 Place the small snowflake right-side down on the art gum eraser and use the small ball stylus to cup it, following the instructions for cupping on page 15. Use the toothpick to apply glue to the snowflake, then set it underneath the sweet pea at the joint between the two sections.

7 To add the leaves, refer to step 5 of the Aster project on page 15.

To make the tendrils

8 Use the small scissors to a cut a strip of bright green cardstock that's approximately ¹⁄₁₆ x 3 inches (1.5 x 76 mm).

9 Using the tweezers, grasp one end of the strip and wrap it around the tweezers. Then slide the piece off the tweezers and open it up slightly. Pick the strip up with the tweezers, dip one end of it into the glue and tuck it into place in the flower.

CARDS

Add an extra dimension to a two-dimensional card with paper flowers. Add decorative paper and trim to accentuate the flowers, or stamp the background of the card so that it complements the paper flowers you're using and adds interest. The card can be shown off in an acrylic box, framed in a shadow box, or displayed on a miniature easel.

TULIP

For many of us, the tulip brings to mind colorful images of Holland. Yet this bright bulb actually originated in Asia. Part of the lily family, this beloved flower occurs in all colors except true blue.

Level of difficulty: ✿ ✿ ✿

Punches for flower and quantity needed
6 large apples for flower [a]
2 medium snowflakes for base of flower [b]
1 small stamen for base of stamen [c]
1 medium pollen for stamen [d]

Punch for leaves and quantity needed
4–8 mega lily petals [e]
(For punch key and individual pieces used, see page 124.)

a   b   c   d   e

Tools and Supplies
Basic Tool Kit (page 11)
Recommended cardstock colors:
Color of your choice for apples
Medium green for medium snowflakes
Black for small stamen and medium pollen
Bright to medium green for petals
Chalk or cake watercolors and water brush for shading (optional)

To make the flower

1 Use the small scissors to cut the stems off all of the apple shapes. If desired, add shading to the apple shapes using the chalk or cake watercolors.

2 Place the apple shapes right-side down on the rubber mat with the large end of each piece pointing away from you. Then use the large ball stylus or rounded end of the molding tool to shape each of the apples, drawing the stylus toward you (refer to page 15 for shaping techniques).

3 Place the snowflakes on the rubber mat and use the large ball stylus to cup both of them, following the instructions for cupping on page 15.

4 Place one of the cupped snowflakes upside down on your middle finger. Then use your free hand and the toothpick to apply glue to the small end of one of the apples. Place the apple on the snowflake so that it covers two of the snowflake's projections. Repeat this step with two more of the apple

shapes until the snowflake projections have been entirely covered. The center of the snowflake should remain open.

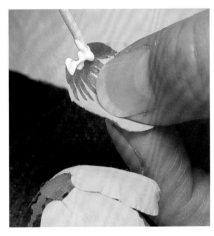

5 Place each of the last three apples shapes over the seams created by the previous row of apples. Let the piece dry for five to 10 minutes.

6 Use the toothpick to apply a small amount of glue to the center of the second cupped snowflake. Then place the snowflake with the apples attached on top of this snowflake.

7 Place the small stamen on the rubber mat and use the small ball stylus to cup it. Use the tweezers to pick up the stamen, then place it inside the tulip, on top of the first snowflake.

8 Use the tweezers to grasp one side of the medium pollen and roll the piece up, leaving a small bit unrolled at the end. Use the toothpick to apply glue to the end, then close the shape up. Grasp the medium pollen at the top with the tweezers, dip the bottom of it into the glue and place it in the center of the tulip, on top of the stamen.

9 Punch the mega lily petals two times to produce four to eight leaves. Add three or four of the leaves to the tulip by referring to step 5 of the Aster project on page 31.

VERBENA

The term verbena comes from the Celtic word ferfaen, *which means "to drive away a stone," a reference to the use of the species* verbena officinalis *as a cure for bladder infections. The verbena blooms from the outside in, so the addition of an unopened flower in the center of the paper version will make it more lifelike.*

Level of difficulty: 🌸 🌸

Punches for flower and quantity needed
4 large cosmos for base of flower [a]
3 medium cosmos for base of flower [b]
12 tiny flowers for flower [c]

Punch for leaves and quantity needed
3–4 medium chestnut leaves [d]

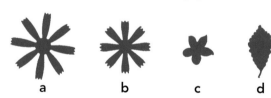

a   b   c   d

Tools and Supplies
Basic Tool Kit (page 11)
Recommended cardstock colors:
  Bright green for large cosmos and 2 medium cosmos
  White, bright pink, purple, or magenta for tiny flowers and 1 medium cosmos
  Bright to medium green for leaves
Pigment ink pens in yellow, green, and a color that matches the tiny flowers
Gel pen in white

To make the flower

1 Use the small scissors to cut the petals of the four large cosmos and the two green medium cosmos in half. Place the large cosmos on the rubber mat and use the medium ball stylus to cup them, following the instructions for cupping on page 15. Then place two of the medium cosmos on the art gum eraser and use the small ball stylus to cup them. Set all of the pieces aside.

2 Use the pigment ink pen to color the third medium cosmos, leaving the tips the color of the cardstock. (Hint: If you punch the tiny flowers from a dark color of cardstock, you may want to use white cardstock for the third medium cosmos. You can then color the stem portion of the cosmos green and use the appropriate pigment ink marker to color the tip area the same color as the tiny flowers.) Use the small scissors to cut the petals of the last cosmos in half, then use the small ball stylus to cup it.

3 Place one of the large cosmos on the rubber mat. Pick up another large cosmos with the tweezers, then use the toothpick to apply glue to the bottom of it and place it on top of the first cosmos. Repeat this step with the remaining large cosmos and the colored, medium cosmos from step 2.

4 Use the toothpick to apply a small amount of glue to the inside of the colored medium cosmos. Set in place on the base layer. Then hold the base of the layered cosmos piece with your index finger and thumb while you fluff the petals with the other hand.

5 Use the white gel pen to make a five-pointed star in the center of one of the tiny flowers, then add a small dot of yellow with the pigment ink pen to the center of the star. Use the small scissors to make cuts that are approximately 1⁄16 inch (1.6 mm) between the petals of the tiny flower. Repeat this step with all of the tiny flowers.

6 Place one of the tiny flowers right-side down on the rubber mat and use the large ball stylus to shape it (refer to page 15 for shaping techniques). Then turn the shape over, place it on the art gum eraser and use the small ball stylus to cup it. Pick the flower up with the tweezers, use the toothpick to apply a small amount of glue to the bottom of it and attach it to one of the petals on the layered cosmos base. Repeat this step to attach all 12 of the tiny flowers to the base, leaving the inside of the piece open.

7 To add the leaves, refer to step 5 of the Aster project on page 31.

VIOLET

This distinctive, tiny flower is also known as the Johnny jump-up because it appears early in the spring garden. Shading the petals of your violet will make it more distinctive, whether you use the flower to fill in your paper bouquet or as the focus of your project.

Level of difficulty:

Punches for flower and quantity needed

4 small ovoid petals [a]

1 small snowflake for base of flower [b]

1 medium ichyou leaf [c]

1 small sparkle for stamen [d]

(For punch key and individual pieces used, see page 124.)

Punch for leaves and quantity needed

3–4 medium birch leaves [e]

a　　b　　c　　d　　e

Tools and Supplies

Basic Tool Kit (page 11)

Recommended cardstock colors:

Lavender, deep purple, yellow, or white for petals and ichyou leaf

Yellow for small sparkle

Medium green for snowflake and birch leaves

Pigment ink marker in purple

Gel pen in yellow for shading dark cardstock

Violet

To make the flower

1 Use the pigment marker (or gel pen) to add shade lines to two of the small ovoid petals and the ichyou leaf.

2 Place the small snowflake on the rubber mat and use the small ball stylus to cup it, following the instructions for cupping on page 15. Set the piece aside.

3 Use the small scissors to trim the ichyou leaf stem, leaving ⅛ inch (3 mm) of stem.

4 Place all four of the ovoid petals and the ichyou leaf on the rubber mat and use the large ball stylus or the half-moon end of the molding tool to shape them (refer to page 15 for shaping techniques).

5 Pinch and bend each of the petals and the ichyou leaf, following the instructions for pinching and bending on page 16.

6 Use the small ball stylus to hold the small snowflake securely on the rubber mat, then use the tweezers to pick up one of the unshaded ovoid petals and dip the pinched end of it into the glue. Place the petal at the top left side of the snowflake. Repeat this step with the second unshaded ovoid petal, placing it at the top right side of the snowflake so that it overlaps the first large petal a bit.

7 Grasp one of the shaded ovoid petals with the tweezers and dip the pinched end of it into the glue. Place the petal on the left side of the snowflake, just below the top left unshaded petal. Repeat this step with the second shaded petal, placing it on the right side, just below the top right unshaded petal.

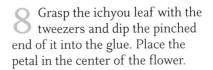

8 Grasp the ichyou leaf with the tweezers and dip the pinched end of it into the glue. Place the petal in the center of the flower.

9 Place the small sparkle on the art gum eraser and use the small ball stylus to cup it. Grasp the sparkle at the top with the tweezers, and use the toothpick to apply a dab of glue to the bottom. Place the sparkle in the center of the flower.

10 Place one of the medium birch leaves on the rubber mat, right-side down. Use the small ball stylus to make a stem line down the center of the leaf. Then turn the leaf over and use the stylus to make vein lines from the stem line out to the edge of the leaf. Shape the leaf as desired (refer to page 15 for shaping techniques). Repeat this step with the remaining leaves. Set the flower in place on your project, then tuck the leaves under it to finish.

COVERED GIFT BOXES

A paper flower added to the front of a covered box that holds jewelry or note cards makes a wonderful keepsake. Covered boxes are available in many shapes and sizes. Give additional decorative elements to the boxes as desired and complete with your paper blossoms.

ZINNIA

A member of the daisy family that originated in Mexico, the zinnia flourishes in warm, sunny climates. It's a popular garden flower, and it tends to attract butterflies.

Level of difficulty: ✿ ✿ ✿

Punches for flower and quantity needed

8 abstract hearts for ray flower [a]

1 large daisy for ray flower [b]

2 silhouette flowers for ray flower [c]

8 medium raindrops for ray flower [d]

2 mayflowers for stamen [e]

4 small suns for stamen [f]

12 five-flower corners for disk flower [g]

(For punch key and individual pieces used, see page 124.)

Punch for leaves and quantity needed

3–4 mega lily petals [h]

(For punch key and individual pieces used, see page 124.)

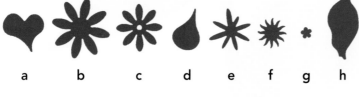

a   b   c   d   e   f   g   h

Tools and Supplies

Basic Tool Kit (page 11)

Recommended cardstock colors:

Bright yellow, red, purple, cream, or various shades of pink for abstract hearts, daisy, silhouette flowers, and raindrops (punch all pieces in the same color)

Contrasting color from those above for mayflowers and small suns

Medium to bright yellow for five-flower corners

Bright green for mega lily petals

To make the flower

1 Use the small scissors to cut the eight abstract hearts in half so that you have 16 petals.

2 Place the large daisy and the two silhouette flowers on the rubber mat and use the large ball stylus to cup each piece, following the instructions for cupping on page 15. Set the pieces aside.

3 Place the medium raindrops on the rubber mat and use the large ball stylus to shape them (refer to page 15 for shaping techniques). Then pinch and bend each of the raindrops, following the instructions for pinching and bending on page 16.

4 Use the small ball stylus to hold the large daisy in place on the rubber mat. Then grasp one of the raindrops with the tweezers, dip the small end of the piece into the glue and attach it to a petal on the large daisy. Repeat this step with all of the raindrops.

5 Place the 16 heart pieces on the rubber mat and use the large ball stylus to shape them. Then use the tweezers to pinch the small end of each piece.

6 Use the large ball stylus to hold one of the silhouette flowers in place on the rubber mat. Grasp one of the heart halves with the tweezers, dip the small end of the piece into the glue and attach it to a petal on the silhouette flower. Repeat this step to fill both silhouette flowers with the heart pieces.

7 Place the large daisy with the raindrops on the rubber mat. Grasp one of the silhouette flowers with the tweezers and use the toothpick to apply a small amount of glue to the bottom of the flower. Set this piece on top of the large daisy, off-setting the petals. Repeat this step with the second silhouette flower, layering it on top of last silhouette flower. Use the tweezers to press down on the center of the piece to secure the layers. These layers create what is called the ray flowers, or outer petals, of the zinnia.

8 Use the small scissors to cut the projections on the may-flowers and the rays on three of the

small suns in half. Place the may-flowers and the three small suns on the rubber mat and use the medium ball stylus to stir them, following the instructions for stirring on page 17.

9 Use the tweezers to pick up one of the mayflowers, then use the toothpick to apply a small amount of glue to the bottom of the piece. Place the mayflower in the center of the layered flower. Repeat this step with the second mayflower, then the three small suns, adding them one at a time.

10 Use the small scissors to cut two-thirds of the way through the center of the fourth small sun. Grasp one side of the sun with the tweezers and roll it into a cone, then use the toothpick to dab a small amount of glue to the opposite side of the sun to secure the shape. Dip the end of the rolled-up sun into the glue and place it in the center of the last layered sun.

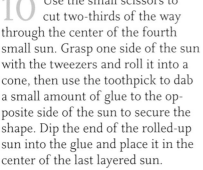

11 Punch the five-flower corner three times to produce a total of 15 flowers. You won't use the largest flower from the punch, so set those pieces aside. Place the remaining 12 small flowers from the five-flower corner punch on the art gum eraser and use the small ball stylus to cup them.

12 Use the tweezers to pick up one of the small flowers, then use the toothpick to apply a small amount of glue to the bottom of the piece. Place the flower on the outer edge of the center of the zinnia. Repeat this step with each of the small flowers from the five-flower corner. These are the tiny disk or inner flowers of the zinnia.

13 Punch the mega lily petals two times to produce eight shapes. You will only use three or four of the petals for the leaves. Use the small scissors to round the ends of three or four of the mega lily petals so that they resemble leaves. Then place one of the leaves right-side down on the rubber mat and use the small ball stylus to create a stem line down the center of the piece. Shape as desired (refer to page 15 for shaping techniques). Repeat this step with each leaf. Then set the flower in place on your project and tuck the leaves under it to finish.

KISSING BALL

Use a five- or six-inch (12.7 or 15.2 cm) polystyrene foam ball for this project. Tear a piece of dark green mulberry paper into small squares, then adhere the pieces to the ball using a decoupage medium or thinned glue. Once the ball is dry, spray it lightly with a floral-scented oil. Use a floral pin to attach a three-inch ribbon loop to the top of the ball, then glue your paper flowers in place, tucking some greenery in between the blossoms. You can hang your kissing ball in a doorway or a window, or place it in a decorative bowl.

PUNCH DIRECTORY

The multi-part punches and theme punches used in this book are shown below in their entirety. Each punch is accompanied by a list of the flowers in which it is used. With certain punches—the super giant moth orchid, or the begonia petals, for instance—you won't need every piece that's punched in order to complete a flower. To find out which pieces you will need for a particular project, look at the diagram of the punch and match the letters to the key underneath the diagram.

MEGA ELONGATED LEAVES

A   Amaryllis
B   Carnation
C   Daffodil
D   Iris

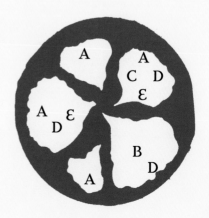

SUPER GIANT BEGONIA PETALS

A   Begonia
     Carnation
B   Gardenia
C   Petunia
D   Rose
E   Pansy

SMALL SPARKLE

A   Violet

5-FLOWER CORNER

A   Zinnia

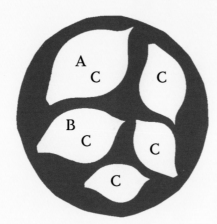

MEGA GIANT DAHLIA PETALS

A   Amaryllis
     Clematis
B   Iris
C   Poinsettia

SUPER GIANT MOTH ORCHID

A   Camellia
     Dogwood
B   Primrose

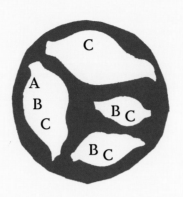

SUPER GIANT LILACS/DAPHNE

A   Camellia

MEGA LILY PETALS

A   Iris
B   Zinnia
C   Tulip

SUPER GIANT VIOLET/IRIS

A   Periwinkle

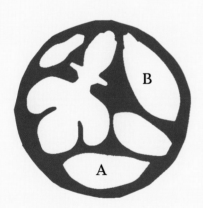

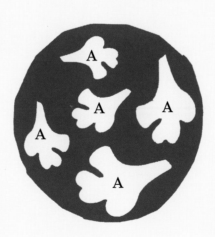

SUPER GIANT CYMBIDIUM ORCHID

A   Daffodil
B.   Rhododendron

MEGA GIANT SNAPDRAGON PETALS

A   Ornamental Kale

MEGA GIANT GARDEN LEAVES

A   Rose

ACKNOWLEDGMENTS

Thank you to: my husband, Chuck; our daughters, Erin Lyn and Kelly Jo; and our sons-in-law, Michael and Matthew. I'm grateful to my mother, Helen, and grandmother, Gladys, for teaching me to appreciate flowers and to be in awe of their beauty and healing powers.

Thanks also to Cheryl Fihn, whose dedication to this craft has allowed me to design and create new blooms, and Gwen Berg, whose vision inspired me to start creating flowers from paper.

My gratitude also goes to Valerie Shrader, Julie Hale, and the staff of Lark Books for taking this journey with me.

ABOUT THE AUTHOR

Susan Tierney Cockburn lives in Seattle, Washington, with her husband, Chuck. They have two daughters, Erin Lyn and Kelly Jo. Susan is a member of the American Horticultural Society and The Blodell Reserve on Bainbridge Island, Washington. The author of *The Paper Garden: Summer Blooms*, Susan also designs a line of rubber stamps; these can be used in conjunction with punches to create dimensional cards. In addition to paper artistry, she enjoys baking, quilting, knitting, and painting.

CRAFT SOURCES

Usually, you can find the supplies you need for making the projects in Lark books at your local craft supply store, discount mart, home improvement center, or retail shop relevant to the topic of the book. Occasionally, however, you may need to buy materials or tools from specialty suppliers. In order to provide you with the most up-to-date information, we have created a listing of suppliers on our website, which we update on a regular basis. Visit us at www.larkbooks.com, click on "Craft Supply Sources," and then click on the relevant topic. You will find numerous companies listed, with the web address and/or mailing address and phone number.

INDEX

Art gum eraser, 11

Basic tool kit, 11

Cardstock, 10

Construction techniques,

    Bending, 16

    Cupping, 15

    Gluing, 18

    Pinching, 16

    Rolling, 19

    Shaping, 15

    Stirring, 17

Garden of Inspiration projects, 29,

    47, 56-57, 75, 81, 111, 119, 123

Glue, 11, 18

Molding tool, 13

Paper craft punches, 11

Punch Directory, 124

Rubber mat, 11

Scissors, 13

Spot color, tools for adding,

    Chalk, 14

    Gel ink pins, 14

    Glitter glue, 14

    Watercolor paints, 14

Stems and veins,

    Creating, 17

Styluses, 12

Tweezers, 13